G000131069

LOCAL GOVERNANCE, DEVELOPMENT AND INNOVATION

Rebuilding Sustainable Local Economies in Ireland

Edited by
Deiric Ó Broin and David Jacobson

GLASNEVIN
PUBLISHING

Published in 2017 by

Glasnevin Publishing
2nd Floor, 13 Upper Baggot Street
Dublin 4, Ireland
www.glasnevinpublishing.com

Papers used by Glasnevin Publishing are from well managed forests and other responsible sources.

ISBN: 978-1-908689-31-3

CONTENTS

LIST OF FIGURES

LIST OF TABLES

ACKNOWLEDGEMENTS

This book is the result of numerous discussions and collaborations with many people at various places over the course of the past four years and these have been immeasurably helpful. The editors would like to thank the members of the Board of Directors and Management Committee of NorDubCo, the School of Law and Government and Business School in Dublin City University, and the School of Transport Engineering, Environment and Planning in the Dublin Institute of Technology for their support, advice and intellectual stimulation.

Deiric Ó Broin would also like to thank the students (past and present) of the LG108 Irish Political System and the LG5007 Policy Challenges modules in the School of Law and Government in DCU, and the students of the BSc Spatial Planning, MSc Local Development and Innovation, MSc Sustainable Development and MSc Urban Regeneration and Development in the School of Transport Engineering, Environment and Planning, DIT for their willingness to engage with so many of the ideas contained in the book. A special debt of gratitude to the women in my life, my late mother who encouraged me to continue my education, Kathleen who put up with many late-night proofing and editing sessions and Sarah who, in her own unassuming way, persuaded me to complete the project so she could watch Elmo on the laptop. Deiric also acknowledges the contributions made by colleagues in the North Dublin Political Economy Discussion Group. These were often challenging but always helpful. Finally, the staff of the Dublin City Library in Cabra were amazing and their colleague, Conor Darcy, who recently passed away, made the library a second home despite all the odd book requests.

David Jacobson would like to express deep appreciation for students and colleagues who, over the years, have forced him to write more clearly, and to think about how to help others to do so, too. These are too numerous to name individually, but one person who must be mentioned is Deiric Ó Broin whose work on projects like the one behind this book inspires admiration. His curiosity, tenacity and productivity are unequalled and I am honoured to be again associated with him as co-editor of a book.

Finally, we would like to thank Jordana Corrigan for her patience and support. There would not be a book without her.

CONTRIBUTORS

Mark Callanan is a lecturer with the Institute of Public Administration. His research interests include local government reform, participative democracy, performance measurement and public sector reform, and the question of economies of scale in local government. Mark has published in a number of international journals, and is the co-editor of the standard textbook on Irish local government. In 2010 he worked on secondment to the Department of Environment, Community & Local Government to carry out work on behalf of the Local Government Efficiency Review Group, which reported to the Irish Government on potential cost savings and efficiencies within the local government sector. Before joining the IPA, Mark worked with Deloitte & Touche in Brussels. He is a graduate of University College Dublin, the College of Europe in Bruges, and University College Cork.

Aidan Culhane is a former special adviser at the Department of Environment, Community and Local Government where he advised on planning, housing, and foreshore issues, and was involved in the preparation of *Putting People First*, the reform programme for local government. He served as a councillor on Dun Laoghaire-Rathdown County Council from 1999 to 2011, and was variously chair of the County Development Board, and the Housing and Planning Strategic Policy Committees. He was also a member of the Dublin Regional Authority and the Southern and Eastern Regional Assembly. He holds a Master's degree in regional and urban planning, and is a qualified town planner.

Declan Curran lectures in Development Economics and Industrial Economics at Dublin City University Business School. Prior to this, he completed a post-doctoral fellowship in the National Institute for Regional and Spatial Analysis (NIRSA), NUI Maynooth. He holds a PhD in Economics from the University of Hamburg. Dr. Curran's research interests focus on the empirics of economic growth across regions and within industry sectors. He has published articles in leading peer reviewed international journals such as *European Planning Studies, World Economy, Applied Economics,* and *Economic Modelling*. He has participated in collaborative research projects at both European and national level, focusing on issues such as knowledge flow within industry clusters, and the role of industry clusters in regional development. His interests in the area of long run economic development have seen him co-edit *Famines in European Economic History: The Last Great European Famines Reconsidered* (Routledge, 2015).

Karl Deeter is the Compliance Manager at Irish Mortgage Brokers (www.mortgagebrokers.ie) and head of client advice at Trinity Accountants and Financial Advisors (www.advisors.ie). He is also a columnist with the Sunday Business Post and the Sun on Sunday as well as a regular contributor to radio, television and newspapers on the topics of mortgages, property, credit, compliance and retail finance.

David Jacobson is Emeritus Professor of Economics at Dublin City University. His research interests include Industrial Economics, Industrial Agglomeration, Industrial Policy, Political Economy and European Integration. He is the author of seven books, including co-author and editor of *Local Dublin, Global Dublin* (2010) and *The Nuts and Bolts of Innovation: New Perspectives on Irish Industrial Policy* (2014) published by Glasnevin Publishing.

Patrick King is the Director of Corporate Affairs and Services at the Society of Chartered Surveyors Ireland. Patrick was previously Head of Public Affairs at Dublin Chamber. He supervised and managed the Chamber's public affairs, publications, media campaigns, communications and a new programme entitled Activating Dublin, a joint initiative of Dublin City Council and Dublin Chamber – as well as other individuals from the private, public and social sectors – aimed at generating growth and employment in the Dublin region. He graduated from Dublin Institute of Technology with a MSc in Strategic Management and from Dublin City University with a MA in International Relations. He previously served as a senior policy analyst at the Institute of International and European Affairs, Dublin.

Lorna Maxwell has worked in the local government sector in both South Dublin County Council and Dublin City Council, specialising in areas of economic and community development. Her work included establishing the County Development Board structure in SDCC, the Economic Development Unit, Creative Dublin Alliance, Innovation

Dublin, and the Docklands SDZ in DCC. In early 2014 Lorna returned to South Dublin County Council as the Director of Corporate Performance and Change Management to lead the HR and Corporate Services departments and the delivery of the local government reform programme within the organisation. Prior to her work in local authorities, Lorna worked in the NGO sector in youth, community and cross-border / anti-sectarian work. Lorna holds a Master's degree in HR Strategies from DCU, a Master's in Public Management from the Institute of Public Administration, a Post-graduate Diploma in Community and Youth Work and an Arts Degree from NUI Maynooth.

Andrew Moore is a Research Associate with NorDubCo and has worked with local government in Dublin on evidenced-based approaches to citizen engagement. Previous to this Andrew worked as a planning and research consultant with national, regional and local government in the UK and has also taught at the University of Liverpool and the Dublin Institute of Technology. As a qualified urban planner, Andrew is interested in spatial approaches to integrating the development and delivery of public policy and the relationship of this to political and public sector management reform. In recent years Andrew has also worked in the private sector, operating as a digital asset management consultant in Dublin's emerging animation and gaming industry. Andrew is also a Creative Producer with O'Brother Productions, producing animated content for television and online platforms.

Hilary Murphy graduated with a BSc in Spatial Planning from DIT in 2004 and took a position as an Urban Planner for the Railway Procurement Agency (RPA), where she worked on the planning and development of light rail projects in Dublin. In 2009 she returned to DIT to undertake an MSc in Sustainable Development. Following her graduation Hilary worked on a rural housing project for the Department of the Environment before joining NorDubCo as a public policy researcher where she spent the next two years undertaking projects relating to local economic development, cleantech, eco-innovation and supporting Dublin City University in a sustainable campus programme. In 2012 she accepted a position with the United Nations Human Settlements Programme (UN-Habitat) and worked as a Sustainable Urban Transport Specialist at the UN Headquarters in

Nairobi, Kenya. Spending two years with UN-Habitat, Hilary worked on international projects in East Africa, South America, India and Nepal. Working closely with both city and national partners, her work focused on urban transport in the context of accessibility, poverty eradication, gender empowerment and participatory planning. In 2014 she joined the United Nations Environment Programme (UNEP) - Division of Technology, Industry and Economics where she continues to work on transport and mobility issues, coordinating the 'Africa Sustainable Transport Forum', an Africa wide initiative to integrate sustainable transport into the region's development and planning processes.

Deiric Ó Broin is Director of NorDubCo, based in Dublin City University, and Senior Research Fellow in the School of Law and Government in DCU where he lectures in Irish politics. In addition he lectures in local development and innovation at the School of Transport Engineering, Environment and Planning in the Dublin Institute of Technology. He is a graduate of the Dublin Institute of Technology (BA [Hons] and LLB), the National College of Industrial Relations (Industrial Relations Management), UCC where he obtained a MBS (Social Enterprise), Keele University, where he completed a MA (Research Ethics) and UCD, where he completed a MA (Politics and Economics) and a PhD (Political Theory). He is Chairperson of the Institute of Economic Development (Ireland Branch), a member of the Executive Committee of the Regional Studies Association (Irish Branch), and Co-Convenor of the Local Government Specialist Group of the Political Studies Association of Ireland.

Colm O'Gorman is Professor of Entrepreneurship at Dublin City University Business School. His research focuses on entrepreneurship and strategy in small and medium sized enterprises (SMEs). Specifically he has studied the growth strategies of SMEs, the nature of managerial work in high growth SMEs, mission statements in SMEs, and internationalisation processes in international new ventures, and in SMEs. He has explored the emergence of high-tech firms in the context of cluster dynamics, including a study of the factors that led to the rapid emergence of the software industry in Ireland during the 1990s. He has examined how inward Foreign Direct Investment impacts on the nature and extent of entrepreneurial activity. His research is published in leading international peer-reviewed journals. He has completed several European Union funded research projects. He is co-author of the annual Global Entrepreneurship Monitor for Ireland.

Seán Ó Riordáin is one of Ireland's leading commentators on local government and local development. He has extensive experience undertaking policy and organisation reviews for the local government sector, the local and community development sector and national departments in Ireland and internationally. He also brings a strong understanding of the policy drivers in the local and national government sectors. Seán is currently contributing to several national policy developments including the reform of local government and local development. Seán is chairman of the Public Policy Advisors Network, the only full service policy advice resource for the Government and Foreign Direct Investment Sector in Ireland. He is also Executive Chairman of Sorhill Advocates Pty. Ltd. in Queensland. In this role he has advised both public and private clients in Brisbane on the regulatory processes required by the international investment community.

Kieran Rose is a Senior Planner in Dublin City Council, and a Commissioner of the Irish Human Rights and Equality Commission. Kieran initiated the vacant land levy by suggesting to Oisin Quinn, as he was about to be elected Lord Mayor of Dublin in 2013 that he might include a vacant land levy as part of his work programme for his year in office. Kieran researched and drafted the detailed submission to Government proposing the vacant land levy (see www.dublincity.ie). The levy is now enacted in the Urban Regeneration and Housing Act 2015. He is an Advisory Board Member of the Center for Theory of Change in New York. He is a graduate of UCC and UCD and an occasional lecturer in those universities and in DIT.

Chris van Egeraat lectures in Economic Geography at the Department of Geography, Maynooth University. He graduated with a Master's degree in Development Geography from Utrecht University and a PhD from DCU Business School. He has worked as a research officer at the Economic and Social Research Institute, a post-doctoral researcher at UCD and as a Research Fellow at the National Institute for Regional and Spatial Analysis (NIRSA), Maynooth. His research interests and publications focus on the production/innovation networks and regional economic development. He has published widely on these topics, including a co-edited volume with Dieter Kogler and Philip Cooke: *Global and Regional Dynamics in Knowledge Flows and Innovation* (Routledge, 2014). He is a research associate of NIRSA and Chair of the Regional Studies Association, Irish Branch.

FOREWORD

Prof. Brian MacCraith, Owen P. Keegan and Paul Reid

This timely volume examines the state of local governance and economic development in the Dublin city region in the aftermath of the most significant reforms of local government in a generation. The implications for the local governments and stakeholders in the city region of changes in our region's economy are discussed, and the potential for innovative approaches to local economic development are critically examined. The contributors offer our elected representatives and communities some considered advice which draws on past experience and the lessons learned from other countries.

In many ways this edited collection is, in itself, a useful example of the type of collaborative venture it espouses. It is based on a seminar series organised by NorDubCo. This is an agency jointly owned by Dublin City Council, Dublin City University, Fingal County Council and three local development agencies operating in North Dublin; it combines expertise and experience from higher education, local government, local development and the private sector. Its primary purpose is the improvement of public policy making in our shared region.

On behalf of Dublin City Council, Dublin City University and Fingal County Council, we are delighted to work with NorDubCo in highlighting the role and importance of co-ordinated public policy interventions and the potential for such collaborative efforts to improve the lives of citizens and communities in the Dublin city region. The key issues faced by the global economy, including the financial crisis and recession, climate change, energy and resource pressures, demographic changes, accelerating technological change, and potential geopolitical change, all have the potential for considerable impact on the Dublin city region. The focus of the volume is thus on the future of public policy in a growing and evolving city region, and the opportunities and limits to both new policy thinking and policy formulation mechanisms. The aim, of course, is to begin a dialogue about these areas of public policy.

We are grateful to the contributors to this volume and especially to the editors, Professor David Jacobson and Dr. Deiric Ó Broin, for organising the original seminar series and for supporting the participants in their contributions to this publication. It is to be hoped that it not only informs the debate about policy making in the Dublin city region but also motivates an engagement with the issues it raises.

Brian MacCraith is President of Dublin City University.
Owen P. Keegan is Chief Executive of Dublin City Council.
Paul Reid is Chief Executive of Fingal County Council.

CHAPTER 1
INTRODUCTION

Deiric Ó Broin and David Jacobson

Background

This book can be seen as a sister volume to *Local Dublin, Global Dublin: Public Policy in an Evolving City Region* (2010) which critically assessed the nature of the relationship between the economy of the Dublin City Region and the key policy-making processes and institutions of governance in the region. A feature of this book, and those that preceded it, is our desire to combine academic insight with the knowledge and experience of those involved in public policy formulation at a variety of levels, and from different practitioner perspectives. We are delighted that so many excellent contributors were able to make an input.

This introductory chapter details the broad economic and political context and focus of the book, broadly reviews the chapter themes, provides some background on the origins of the book and finally, suggests the possible contribution the book can make.

Setting the Economic and Political Context

Ó Riain (2014:4-5) insightfully outlines the origins of Ireland's economic crises. Building on the earlier work of the National Economic and Social Council he details the multifaceted aspects of it. At the core was a financial crisis arising from "an unholy combination of property speculation by developers, reckless lending by banks and a lack of governmental oversight and regulation [that] created a property and banking bubble" (2014:4). A fiscal crisis arose as, on the income side, property-linked tax revenues shrank and on the expenditure side the public finances struggled to meet the costs of bailing out the banks. This was reinforced by an economic crisis as competitiveness waned and domestic demand collapsed. The financial, fiscal and economic crises "drove a major social crisis based on negative equity and mortgage arrears, cutbacks in public services and disastrous rises in unemployment" (2014:5). In turn these created a reputational crisis as international lenders were reluctant to finance government debt. This culminated in a EU-IMF bailout in November 2010. Finally these crises "hastened and were reinforced by [another], broader crisis of political capacity, solidarity and action" (2014:5).

In addition to the various legal, institutional, regulatory and policy responses being devised and implemented at national level, this catastrophic set of inter-related dynamics raised many questions for local public governance arrangements and local economies. As academics and practitioners, the contributors ask whether we can learn from the crises; remake our local economic and political systems to obviate a recurrence; develop resilience in our key systems; and learn from other countries' experience to help in this process of improvement.

While acknowledging the terrible human costs of the crises in Ireland it is important to note how unusual this period is. As Merrett and Walzer note, "we live in paradoxical times" (2004:3). We have witnessed the dominance of laissez-faire policymakers advocating the expansion of global markets through free trade agreements (Cohen, 1995) and the financialisation[1] of many economies (Fine *et al.*, 2013). Consequently, local producers and workers must increase their efficiency and scale of operations to compete. At the same time many advocates of the market promote the merits of personal responsibility, community and local control. These conflicting policy prescriptions confront social and economic development practitioners with a "conundrum" (Merrett and Walzer, 2004:3). How can communities composed of locally-owned businesses, including farms, local public service providers and "place-bound consumers" (2004:3) compete against intense global economic pressures that undermine the social and civic relations that many take for granted? As we emerge, slowly for many, from the recent crises we have had an opportunity to reflect on how we move forward, what and how to rebuild, and how to ensure

---

[1] Financialisation is a relatively new term and has its roots primarily in heterodox economics and Marxist political economy (Fine, 2007:2-4) although it is increasingly adopted by orthodox economists. It has also been understood in a number of different ways. First, at the most casual level, it refers to the expansion and proliferation of financial markets over the past thirty years, during which the ratio of global financial assets to global GDP has risen three times, from 1.5 to 4.5 (Palma, 2009). Second, financialisation has been associated with the expansion of (and invention of new) speculative assets at the expense of mobilising and allocating investment for real activity. Third, it is the increasing predominance of shareholder value as sole determinant in corporate governance. Fourth, at a systemic level, financialisation is the increasing power of financiers and financial markets over the rest of the economy and even government policy. This is reflected in such phrases as "we are constrained by the markets" (See also Foroohar, 2016).

that the result is sustainable local economies with appropriate governance arrangements. We argue that the experience of the crises should not deflect public policy makers from the medium- to long-term focus. The costs have been terrible and often borne by those least equipped to do so but they should be appropriately contextualized. As O'Hagan and Newman (2014:xii) note, policy makers have to remain aware of the distractions of:

> short-term gyrations of financial markets or predictions of imminent doom or boom. The world is a much more complex place. Things come in cycles; and how easily people forget the past, even the immediate past. That is the real danger that confronts Ireland in the years ahead.

A critical response to the crises by the government elected in early 2011 was to initiate a broad review of the existing local government system. This was a significant task involving a number of elements, some of which had already been initiated:

- Local Government Efficiency Review Group[2];
- Inter-Departmental Group on Property Tax[3];

---

[2] The Local Government Efficiency Review Group was established in December 2009 to carry out an independent review of the cost base, expenditure of and numbers employed in local authorities. The Group, which presented its report to the Minister in July 2010, made 106 recommendations (in effect a menu of options for consideration to be pursued in the short, medium and long terms) and identified a range of efficiency savings and other revenue options. These totalled €511m (€346m in efficiencies and €165m in improved cost recovery and revenue-raising). A number of the recommendations required legislative change, or action supported by agencies in the public sector other than within the local government system.

One of the key recommendations of the Report was the establishment of an Implementation Group to drive and oversee the implementation of relevant recommendations of the Report. The Implementation Group with independent chair Pat McLoughlin and private sector expertise was established in April 2011. The Implementation Group was asked to oversee and advise on the delivery of efficiency gains and savings in areas such as shared services, procurement, value for money and audit in the local government sector. It was asked to focus particularly on driving key recommendations of the Report that will remove costs and yield earliest financial savings for the sector and the economy generally.

[3] In January 2012, the Minister for Environment, Community and Local Government, Mr. Phil Hogan TD, established an Inter-Departmental Group on Property Tax under the

- Alignment of Local Government and Local Development[4];
- Putting People First – Action Programme for Effective Local Government[5];
- Replacing City/County Enterprise Boards[6];
- A variety of local government merger and boundary amendment initiatives, including Limerick City and County, North Tipperary and South Tipperary, Waterford City and County and Cork City and County;
- Local Electoral Area Boundary Committee.

The review and a number of related actions led to the passing of the Local Government Reform Act, 2014. This legislation led to the largest number of reforms in Irish local governance in a generation and the ramifications of the reforms are still being considered, in particular in the area of economic development. For example the act introduced a statutory-based 'Local Economic and Community Plan' (LECP) as a companion to the existing spatial planning city/county development plan. The first of these LECPs was launched in mid-2016 and it remains unclear the significance or impact that they will have on existing policy procedures and patterns of implementation.

This book can be situated in this context. It is the product of a reflective process, moderated in part by academics, but driven and shaped by practitioners. As editors we worked to give the contributors the time, support and an opportunity to reflect on their roles so that

---

independent chairmanship of Dr. Don Thornhill. This Group was tasked with considering the design of a property tax, to be approved by Government, to replace the Household Charge. A local property tax was introduced in 2013.

[4] The Steering Group for the Alignment of Local Government and Local Development was established by the Minister for the Environment, Community and Local Government, Mr. Phil Hogan TD, in September 2011. The group submitted its final report in March 2012. The Steering Group was given the following Terms of Reference:
- Review the role of Local Government in Local and Community Development;
- Review the role and contribution of Local and Community Development programmes in order to determine the scope for greater synergy with Local Government; and
- Make recommendations on how the alignment of Local Government and Local and Community Development should be progressed.

[5] The report was published on 16 October 2012 and sets out a wide range of reforms for local government, encompassing local authority functions, structures, funding, performance and governance.

[6] County Enterprise Boards (Dissolution) Act 2014.

they might, in future, engage with their organisations and develop new approaches to shared problems.

Themes

This book draws together contributions from academics and practitioners in the public policy, spatial planning, economic development, politics, business representative, finance, local government and local development sectors in Ireland and the chapters are grouped into three broad themes relating to form, finance and function.

The first theme is the nature, structure and governance (the "form") of local government and local development in Ireland. Four separate chapters address selected aspects of this theme. The authors all have direct experience in the areas about which they write but they have addressed their topics with due consideration for the academic literature. From spatial considerations in the construction of an administrative infrastructure for local government (Chapter 2), examinations of the role of city government (Chapter 3) and how to determine decisions on local development (Chapter 4). This first section of the book provides a strong foundation for any scholar or politician interested in becoming involved in the research, development and implementation of policy on local areas and their political governance and economic development.

In the second theme of the book the focus is on finance, the authors of the three chapters in this section again have in their backgrounds a combination of academic study and practical application, resulting in thoughtful work on local property tax (Chapter 5), on vacant land tax (Chapter 6) and on the potential for the National Asset Management Agency (NAMA) to contribute to local economic development (Chapter 7). Not all the work in these chapters is in agreement, either with policy implemented by government or with each other's arguments. The section is therefore all the more important in the context of the current (2016) political reconsideration of how to generate local fiscal revenues.

We have used the term "function" to describe the third theme addressed in this book. We use this term in the sense of how local economic development might be approached. The possibilities considered in the four chapters in this section are not necessarily mutually exclusive. Enterprise zones (Chapter 8) may even be enhanced by an acknowledgement of the importance of local government as the setting for local economic development (Chapter 9). In general this section can be seen as offering different combinations of ways of achieving the goals of sustainable local development. The first two chapters are written by people who perhaps more than any others actively straddle the worlds of research and application, of academic work and policy advice and productive practice. The other two chapters are the result of academic collaborations among people who spend most of their time in academic institutions. However, these are not "ivory tower" academics, as is clearly evident from the practical issues addressed, namely the development of a particular modern sub-sector (biotech) (Chapter 10), and ways of combining sustainability with the traditional concerns of industrial development (Chapter 11).

Origins

The book has its genesis in the annual Martin McEvoy Conference run by NorDubCo in Dublin City University (DCU). The conferences were organised and led by Deiric Ó Broin (NorDubCo) and David Jacobson (DCU) in late 2012 and reflect a key aspect of NorDubCo's mission in the region, and the key role played by the university as a generator of knowledge.

NorDubCo is a coalition of public stakeholders established in 1996 to advance social, economic and civic innovation North Dublin region. Its members currently include Dublin City University, Dublin City Council, Fingal County Council, Dublin Northwest Area Partnership and Blanchardstown Area Partnership.

The motive force behind NorDubCo's establishment was the shared belief that local government, local development agencies, the local university, local civil society organisations and local communities working together could make a difference to the region. At that time a very specific set of challenges faced the region and NorDubCo was configured to address those challenges. The period of prolonged economic growth and subsequent crises has changed many of the issues facing the region. In some cases, old issues are at least partially resolved or no longer as problematic. In others, changes in the economy have created a completely new set of issues to be addressed by the members of NorDubCo.

Throughout this period, NorDubCo has worked to advance social, economic and civic innovation in the region. As part of this it has worked to create a positive vision for community and working life for the region, a vision that seeks to embrace all of the region's communities. In operationalising this vision, NorDubCo's work has a number of distinct objectives. Of particular relevance is its contention, reflecting that of our stakeholders, that the region needs to develop a more inclusive policy debate and promote new thinking to influence the social, economic and civic environment.

In working towards these objectives NorDubCo works with representatives from a wide variety of civil society organisations, the business community, local government, the local development sector, public representatives (both local and national), education establishments (secondary, further and higher), the media, and state and semi-state institutions. The development of these relationships allows NorDubCo to facilitate a broad range of policy discussions among various stakeholders.

Underpinning these efforts is the belief that a fundamental challenge facing North Dublin is to overcome barriers to shared decision–making. This requires a climate conducive to negotiated governance, that is the involvement of variable networks of communities, civil society actors and other stakeholders in the relevant policy formulation and decision-making processes. Developing this form of governance involves addressing the issues of building and sustaining a social and civic environment facilitative and supportive of such a process. Such inclusive decision-making must also be responsive to both the long-term and immediate needs of communities, as well as the infrastructural and developmental requirements of enterprise in the region. It requires paying particular attention to inclusion and participation of the most disadvantaged.

As a contribution to the development of such a form of negotiated governance NorDubCo devised a Public Dialogue Programme in conjunction with our colleagues in Dublin City University. This programme of activities is based on an understanding that civic engagement is the foundation of a thriving, vibrant civil society and a recognition that a space for dialogue about issues of public importance is often lacking. It is our earnest hope that NorDubCo's Public Dialogue Programme contributes to the addressing of these issues.

An important component of our programme is the annual Martin McEvoy Conference. The conferenece commemorates the former chairperson of NorDubCo. Martin served as Chairperson of NorDubCo from 1999 until 2007 and his commitment was both unceasing and constructive. He always played a pivotal role in our work. Whether it was sailing, his beloved Suttonians, business or local development, he was professional, dedicated and committed. He served with the Tolka Area Partnership as chairperson for their first five years and in the process supported hundreds of local people in setting up businesses or finding worthwhile employment. Martin was a founding member and former President of the North Dublin Chamber of Commerce and in addition he was an active member of the Council of the Dublin Chamber of Commerce. He also chaired the Fingal Enterprise Board, again supporting scores of new businesses to get started and grow. He served as chairperson of two boards of community initiatives in Corduff and Ladyswell in West Dublin. One provided a support service to elderly residents in the area and the other oversaw the establishment of a local youth and sports facility. All of this was after he had officially retired. Martin represented everything that was positive about the business community in North Dublin. He believed it was his community of which he was an integral part and he should serve as best he could in helping it develop. In a very practical way he believed in the common good and worked for it in a variety of ways, often with thanks and recognition, often without.

As an organisation we were diminished by Martin's untimely death. We lost a great friend and colleague with his passing. He had time for everyone and treated everyone equally. He will be remembered fondly for the genuine person that he was and it was a privilege for those of us fortunate enough to work with him. As a way of commemorating Martin, NorDubCo's board of directors decided to rename our annual conference in his memory.

We feel it was appropriate because, in addition to his practical commitment to help build the capacity of communities, Martin McEvoy was intensely curious about ideas and thought the conference, and its audience of politicians, students, public servants and community activists engaged in debate and, more often than not, disagreement, was a great addition to the region. As he often observed, over a coffee after a particularly intense debate, 'this type of discussion changes the way people see problems'.

We hope to continue in this vein for many years to come. The conference has been running since 2001 and each year attempts to address issues of contemporary concern. As noted earlier, the aim is not just to present information but to develop a dialogue between presenter and audience and amongst the audience itself, in order to develop a fuller, more robust and shared understanding of the various issues under discussion. It was in this context that David Jacobson and Deiric Ó Broin devised the parameters for the chapters in this volume. Three chapters were not part of the conference but we included them as we feel they add particular value. Culhane's provides a rich and contemporary set of practitioner insights and King and Deeter's provides a very useful framework for analysing many of the key components of the various local taxation initiatives recently proposed, implemented and reconsidered. Rose's chapter details a very particular approach to developing an appropriate local taxation base and has been the subject of considerable debate by policy makers.

David Jacobson and Deiric Ó Broin, June 2017

CHAPTER 2
LOCAL GOVERNMENT AND TERRITORIAL REFORM: DOES SIZE MATTER?

Mark Callanan

Introduction

The question of restructuring or reconfiguring local government boundaries has become a matter of some debate, in the context of broader local government reforms and indeed public sector reform more generally. One dimension of approaches to public service reform has emphasised the amalgamation of public bodies. This includes the mergers of several state agencies, as well as the amalgamation of regional health boards into a single Health Service Executive. The common label for reforms such as these is 'rationalisation'.

In the local government arena the topic of reconfiguring the territorial structure of Ireland's local authorities has been reflected in several recent proposals, and in the abolition and amalgamation of local government units that took effect in 2014, reducing the number of local authorities from 114 to 31.

Over time a number of other jurisdictions have implemented territorial reforms aimed at restructuring local government boundaries. During the 1960s and 1970s, there were dramatic reductions in the number of local authorities in countries such as Britain, Denmark, Germany, the Netherlands, Belgium and Sweden (Sharpe, 1995; Vetter and Kersting, 2003). More recently, amalgamations of significant numbers of local authorities have been implemented or proposed in places such as Northern Ireland, New Zealand, several Canadian provinces and Australian states, and (for a second time) Denmark (Baldersheim and Rose, 2010).

Debates over the relationship between structure and performance are arguably one of the oldest in public management (Andrews, 2010). This chapter focuses specifically on the question of territorial reform in Ireland: that is proposals for reforming the structures and in particular the geographical configuration of local government areas. The next section that follows briefly outlines the present structures. The third section presents some earlier and contemporary proposals, up to and including the proposals in the *Putting People First* action programe, published in 2012, thus placing the current territorial reforms in their historical context. The fourth section suggests a number of reasons for the resilience of local government structures, while the fifth section presents the suggested rationale for territorial reform, based on official reports and reviews, which typically point to the desire to reduce the costs of, and enhance efficiency in, local government. The sixth section reviews the extensive international, and some initial Irish research into the relationship between local government size and efficiency. The final section offers some concluding remarks.

Territorial Government in Ireland – Town, County, City, Region

The territorial structure of local government in Ireland has, in comparative terms, been remarkably resilient. Until 2014, there had been no system-wide reorganisation of local government boundaries since 1898. Contrast this with countries such as New Zealand or Denmark where governments have sometimes introduced quite drastic re-drawing of the local government 'map', very often with a view to reducing the number of local authorities. Other countries, such as the Netherlands have implemented more incremental territorial reforms of local government structures over a period of many years. Scotland could arguably be considered a case of hyper-territorial reform, having reconfigured its local government structures no less than four times since the late nineteenth century (in 1889, 1929, 1975 and 1996)! Territorial reform of this nature seems to have been part and parcel of the local government reform 'package' in these jurisdictions. But not so in Ireland, at least until relatively recently.

As the Devlin Report (1969:15) put it, "although local government in Ireland has some ancient antecedents, it is, in its present form, largely a nineteenth century creation". As with many countries in Europe, Irish local government has medieval origins, although the actual establishment of the contemporary local government structures is based on the adoption of the Local Government (Ireland) Act 1898. This pre-independence legislation, adopted by the Westminster Parliament, provided for the establishment in Ireland of county councils and maintenance of the city and town system which had undergone reforms earlier under the Municipal Reform Act of 1840. The territorial structures established by the 1898 Act are still the fundamental basis for today's local government areas, albeit with a few changes made here and there. It is important to emphasise that this is not to suggest that there has been no change in local government for over a century – far from it. But change seems to be path dependent in terms of some issues that have been on the agenda for change, and other issues which have typically been off the agenda and taken as a given – amongst the latter we can arguably include territorial structures (Callanan, 2007). At various stages reforms have been implemented, affecting some key features of local governance. These include reforms such as transfer of functions (usually taking responsibilities from local government), changes in local government revenue sources, the introduction of management systems (partly inspired by US models), modernisation of service delivery, and development of new structures designed to facilitate greater participation in local government decision-making. However, territorial structures seem to have been relatively immune to change, or at least have not been a political priority, until now. Thus reforms have tended to be bounded, and have taken place within a relatively non-negotiable framework in terms of existing local government areas (Callanan and MacCarthaigh, 2008).

Separate from, but closely linked to, the local government system are the regional assemblies (and previously the regional authorities). The original impetus for the establishment of these structures was largely external via the European Union, and this perhaps reflects the pragmatic approach to territorial reform at regional level (Moylan, 2011; Hayward, 2010; Quinn, 2009). Their responsibilities are quite restricted, and do not involve direct service provision, thus making them rather invisible to the general public. This is illustrated by their tiny staffing complements – just 76 staff across all regional authorities and regional assemblies in 2012, compared to over 28,000 staff working in local authorities (Government of Ireland, 2012).

Proposals for Change
For the most part, territorial reform of local government has received scant attention from reformers. Where proposals have been made for change, they are typically addressed in passing and in the context of wider reforms of the local government system. For example, the Devlin Report on public service reform and reorganisation noted that, while the appropriate size of local government was outside of its remit, there were differences of opinion on the utility of the county as an adequate unit of administration, with some arguing that local authorities need to be more local and others suggesting that there is a case for larger regional structures for some areas of service provision.

12

A 1971 Government White Paper on *Local Government Reorganisation* considered the question of local government size, concluding that it was not possible to identify an optimal size of a local authority, either for all or for particular services. Equally, the White Paper suggested that specifying minimum or maximum sizes for local authorities was not likely to be especially helpful, as there was inevitably going to be an element of trade-off between different considerations, including economies of scale, local democracy, financial capacity, ability to employ skilled staff, and organisational and management problems that can arise with larger organisations. Ultimately, the paper recommended that local government areas should not be larger "than is necessary to enable functions to be carried out effectively ... without, at the same time, becoming too remote from the people" (Government of Ireland, 1971:17).

The logical extension of this argument could have been a two-tier sub-national governance structure, which was a common feature of local government territorial reform in many developed countries in the 1960s and 1970s, and which also reflected an international interest in regional planning at the time. This would have allowed for a distribution of responsibilities for certain services to larger regional structures where economies of scale and coordination was deemed a particular priority, with other services, particularly those that entailed direct contact with the public, provided at a more accessible local or district level.

However, the White Paper made the case for essentially retaining the county system as the primary level of sub-national government. It conceded that the county structure had its flaws and that if county structures were being mapped for the first time they would look different to those we have inherited. Ultimately it argued that the county structure was "powerfully supported by local sentiment and tradition", that counties were generally large enough to be viable service providers without being too large as local authorities and that, therefore, the county should remain "the basic unit of local government" (Government of Ireland, 1971:25).

A subsequent report on local government management and staff structures, commissioned by the government on foot of the White Paper, went further. It argued that, from an administrative efficiency perspective, integrating the towns and county structures to create "a unitary system based on the counties alone would be most economical and most effective. Even then, many [counties] are rather small to support a full complement of staff of the necessary calibre to carry out the wide range of services involved" (McKinsey, 1971:4).

The Barrington Report (1991) did not consider a radical overhaul of the county /city structure. It noted both the extent of county loyalties and the fact that government policy was to retain the county structure as the basic framework for local government. The report did however propose the division of the old Dublin county council into three county council areas. The report's recommendations also included placing regional structures on a statutory footing, and an overhaul of sub-county structures

The 1996 White Paper, *Better Local Government*, which became the basis for a number of fundamental reforms of local government, was noteworthy in that the issue of territorial reform was largely glossed over. It did point out that "existing county/city structures are suitable for most local authority functions and will remain the primary units of local government. The historical counties themselves attract strong traditional loyalties" (Government of Ireland, 1996:71-72). Ultimately, the *Better Local Government* paper argued that "structural change should be avoided at this point pending the introduction of the new funding system and the potential strengthening of the management and human resource dimension" (Ibid., 66).

While the 2008 Green Paper on Local Government had subsidiarity as one if its guiding principles, again the specific topic of territorial reform received only brief, and largely, passing references. One option that was mentioned was establishing unitary authorities in gateway areas such as Limerick, Waterford and Sligo, involving the merger of county council and city/ borough councils in these areas, while also respecting county boundaries. It again referred to the primacy of county and city councils within the local government system, suggesting that "the county basis of local government in Ireland remains sacrosanct" (Government of Ireland, 2008:30). In relation to boundary changes, it noted the particular emotional affinity to county boundaries and that "proposals to alter county administrative boundaries [are] politically divisive, highly emotive, and difficult to resolve [and] lead to significant public resistance" (Ibid., 111).

The first radical break with the past arguably came with the proposals of the McCarthy Report in 2009. The report attracted considerable media attention and controversy given the many radical proposals made by it to curb public expenditure across all areas of the public service, proposals which were primarily driven by the need to reduce the deficit in the public finances that had become manifest by that time. Amongst its suggestions was the proposed abolition of all town councils to create a single-tier local government structure, along with a reduction of the number of county and city councils from 34 to 22 (McCarthy Report, 2009). It also proposed the abolition of regional authorities. The assumptions that underpinned the report were, for the most part, vague and unstated. But one implicit assumption running throughout, and reflected in the proposals to amalgamate not just local authorities but also state agencies, was savings arising from economies of scale. Rather than full-scale amalgamation, the Local Government Efficiency Review Group report (2010) suggested that a number of county/city councils be paired as joint administrative areas (i.e. with a common management and staff pool serving two county/city council areas), and that certain responsibilities in planning, roads and housing be transferred from town council level to county council level.

The proposals in the 2012 *Putting People First* Action Programme involved considerable territorial reform of local government structures, particularly at sub-county and regional level, as well as a limited number of mergers of county/city councils. The Programme argued that "a strong, rational, cohesive and modern structural 'architecture' … is fundamental to advancing the strategic aims of operational efficiency and representational effectiveness and accountability, enabling local government to perform its current role as effectively as possible, and improving its capacity to take on new functions" (Government of Ireland, 2012:46).

Under the Programme town and borough councils were dissolved and replaced by 'municipal districts' based on town and hinterland, a territorial structure that reflects the norm across most European countries. The municipal districts are generally based on existing town councils and other urban areas that previously did not have local government status. Separate arrangements exist for city councils and local authorities in the Dublin area which may establish area committees. Councillors at local elections are elected firstly to the 'municipal district'. There are a number of these districts in each county area. The same councillors come together with councillors from other municipal districts in the county to meet in plenary as the county council. Thus elected representatives have a dual function –

representing the wider county, and representing the district that they are elected to.

Certain reserved functions may be exercised at municipal district level (indicative examples include powers to make bye-laws in areas such as litter, parking, traffic calming and speed limits on local roads and the power to make housing services and homelessness plans or local area plans). The county council may also decide that other reserved functions be addressed at municipal district level. The county council remains as the budgetary authority, with the power to determine local rates and taxes, although the option may also be given to allocate 'block' funding budgets to municipal districts through the county council budget. A single county-wide administrative structure supports both the county council and the municipal districts in the area.

The Action Programme echoes earlier policy papers in stating that because "there is an established citizen allegiance to the county ... the longstanding policy whereby city and county authorities form the core element of local government is still valid" (Government of Ireland, 2012:76). It also contends that, given the lack of regional identity in Ireland, and that larger structures would be less conducive to citizen representation, "there is not a convincing case for configuration of local government into regionally based political or representational entities" (Government of Ireland, 2012:76). That said, the Action Programme proposes the retention of relatively weak regional structures, on the basis of a consolidation of the eight regional authorities and two regional assemblies into three new regional assembly areas with similar responsibilities.

Explaining the Resilience of Territorial Structures

Until 2014, no major overhaul of local government structures had been implemented, and the significant changes introduced in 2014 have largely retained the county and city structure, and in particular have respected traditional county boundaries. Even *proposals* for change have been spasmodic and have tended to focus on changes at sub-county level, rather than changes to county/ city structures. There also seems to have been a reluctance to engage in meaningful territorial reform at regional level to reflect contemporary population, housing and commuter patterns of urban development and the evolution of 'city regions' which can act as centres of investment and drivers of economic growth for their hinterlands (see for example Ó Broin, 2010; Williams *et al.*, 2010).

One explanation for the resilience of local government territorial structures is the strong affinity of most Irish citizens with county boundaries (Callanan and MacCarthaigh, 2008). Many sporting, political and social groups tend to be organised on a county basis. Callanan (Callanan *et al.*, 2007) argues that "revision of local government boundaries which directly challenge deeply-rooted territorial identities have never been seriously considered" (2007:133). Territorial reforms and even specific proposals for boundary reforms, when they run up against county allegiances, seem to quickly run into the sand. Objectively, there may be strong grounds for re-drawing boundaries, particularly where contemporary cities and towns have outgrown their historic boundaries, and where urban development has had a spill-over effect into neighbouring local authority areas. But when such proposals for boundary extension involve the change of a county boundary, local opposition tends to quickly emerge; witness the fate of proposed boundary extensions of Limerick city into Clare, or Waterford city into Kilkenny, or Carlow town into Laois. Clearly, parts of south Clare, south Kilkenny and south-eastern Laois have become part of the natural hinterland of Limerick, Waterford and Carlow respectively, but proposals to alter boundaries to reflect that reality have fallen foul of local preferences. Proposed changes to Dáil constituencies which do not respect county boundaries also tend to spark public resistance (Daly, 2001).

The selection of particular city and county councils for amalgamation in the *Putting People First* proposals also suggests that maintaining traditional county structures was a key consideration. Proposing that mergers be confined to Limerick city and county, Waterford city and county, and the previous two Tipperary local government areas, suggests that a reluctance to trespass on traditional county affinities was the primary criterion in making this choice. Indeed the Action Programme itself states, that while further territorial reform at county level is not ruled out for the future, "amalgamation of different county authorities would not be appropriate in view of strongly established county identity" (Government of Ireland, 2012:85). The Action Programme also points to the short to medium-term organisational and service disruption that would arise in any wide-scale restructuring process at county/city level, which would have to be

17

considered relative to potential longer term benefits from scale efficiencies.

A second possible explanation for the resilience of local government structures is the typically strong intra-party links between local councillors (at town, county and city level) and national politicians. Territorial reforms typically incorporate an alteration of the number of local councillors, or at the very least a change in electoral boundaries where local councillors may have invested many years in building up a profile. As Kenny (2003) points out, the cohort of local councillors can be regarded as a standing army, the 'footsoldiers' and canvassers for national politicians when it comes to general elections. This makes it highly unlikely that ministers of any party would be naturally predisposed to alienating this group.

A final explanation may lie in the lack of public debate over appropriate territorial structures in the context of wider debates into public service reform. As Moylan (2011) notes, governance in Ireland operates largely on a functional rather than a territorial basis. Strategies emanating from government departments are, for the most part, resolutely sectoral in focus, emitting a subconscious faith in uniformity, and tend to neglect any territorial dimension or consideration of regional or local distinctiveness. Given that a functional rather than a territorial approach dominates national strategies, the case for territorial reform is arguably lessened. Why invest financial and political capital in altering territorial structures when the predominant approach to public policy is to ignore these structures?

Rationales and Economies of Scale

The conventional debate on territorial reform holds that smaller local authorities are more democratic by virtue of being closer to the citizen, while larger local authorities can benefit from economies of scale. There are echoes of these somewhat intuitive assumptions in the limited discussions that have taken place on territorial reform in Ireland. For example, the trade-off between local democracy and efficiencies and economies of scale seemed to be the main point of debate in discussions over the proposed extension or abolition of the town councils in the 2008 Green Paper on Local Government Reform (Government of Ireland, 2008: 70-73).

Reducing the number of local authorities became synonymous with reducing costs – this is reflected in some of the more recent proposals for reform, as well as in the limited media attention given to territorial reform (see for example Drennan, 2011; Power, 2012). Such sentiments were built on a conventional wisdom which holds that: inefficiency and wastefulness can be 'illustrated' by the fact that before the 2014 reforms there were 34 county and city councils (114 local authorities if one includes town councils) for a country with a population of just over 4.5 million, thus concluding that there were 'too many'[7]. This 'problem', having been identified, could be remedied through the merging or amalgamation of local authorities, which should reduce duplication and allow for savings through economies of scale. It is a simple, and, indeed at first sight, compelling argument to make, based as it is on intuitive logic[8].

The appropriate scale of local government and the question of economies of scale have been themes bandied about rather casually in discussions and considerations around territorial reforms over the decades. As outlined above, the 1971 White Paper considering local government size suggested a trade-off between economies of scale and a range of other variables (Government of Ireland, 1971). The McKinsey report on local government staffing suggested that economies of scale tended to lead to higher proportionate costs in smaller counties compared to larger counties, both for administrative overhead costs, and for the costs of providing services such as fire and motor tax (McKinsey, 1971).

The 1996 *Better Local Government* White Paper argued that some more complex services "now demand a scale well beyond the county level" which justified either transferring some responsibilities to national agencies or a more regional approach involving inter-local authority co-operation (Government of Ireland, 1996:69). The 2008 Green Paper, in considering the role of town councils, argued that

---

[7] This assertion does not stand up to scrutiny, at least as far as international comparators are concerned. In countries of a similar population size to Ireland, such as New Zealand or Denmark (even after significant territorial reforms), the number of local authorities is considerably larger than of Irish county and city councils. In fact, with the sole exception of Britain, on a per capita basis Ireland has by some distance the fewest local authorities in the developed world (Callanan *et al.*, 2014).

[8] One limitation of much current political and public discourse on local government reform in Ireland is the exclusive focus on the need for savings and efficiencies (and implied 'waste'). This narrative ignores the evidence of a funding gap identified by Indecon (2005) and numerous other studies on local government financing in Ireland. Space does not permit consideration of this issue in detail within the confines of this chapter, but it is important to draw attention to it.

"town councils are not generally of a scale to enable them to perform all of the complex social, environmental and infrastructural functions required of modern local government" (Government of Ireland, 2008:65).

The Local Government Efficiency Review Group in advocating joint administrative areas to service multiple county/city councils, considered the variation in size of county and city councils, suggesting that "smaller counties cannot be expected to achieve minimum efficient scale in several areas, regardless of how well they work" (Government of Ireland, 2010:61). Economies of scale are also instanced in the report as the basis for moving to shared service arrangements between multiple local authorities in areas such as IT, recruitment, procurement, and technical support services in roads and water protection among others.

The 2012 *Putting People First* proposals also reflected on size and scale issues. The document acknowledged that "the quantification of economies of scale within local government is a complex matter due, among other things, to different scale characteristics of different activities and the multi-functional nature of local authorities" (Government of Ireland, 2012:11). It suggested that the case for devolution is strongest where centralised provision of services will not yield substantial economies of scale, or where a shared service approach between local authorities can achieve sufficient scale effects. The chapter dealing with the abolition of town councils argued that "while the relationship between scale and efficiency can vary with different functions, a multiplicity of small authorities is not generally conducive to operational efficiency, especially in the case of services that are subject to economies of scale or which require specialised resources or expertise" (Government of Ireland, 2012:49). Economies of scale are also mentioned in the context of the amalgamation of county/city councils in Limerick, Tipperary and Waterford, the transfer of water services to a national agency, and in the context of moving to a single administrative and staffing structure between county and sub-county levels.

International and Domestic Evidence
Efficiency (albeit broadly defined) has been a driving force and motivation for territorial reform of local government in many jurisdictions (see for example Baldersheim and Rose, 2010). The

question of economies of scale in local government and the link between efficiency and local authority size are well researched areas internationally. Several hundred articles, chapters and papers have been devoted to the topic, with empirical research spanning North America, Europe and Australasia. And yet, notwithstanding the large volume of studies, the findings are rather inconclusive.

Proponents of territorial reform and amalgamation based on economies of scale, often overlook the fact that economic theory also recognises *dis*economies of scale, and limits to economies of scale (Sharpe, 1995). As production increases, the challenges, complexities and costs of managing production processes may become greater than the gains from increasing returns. Thus there are non-linear relationships between costs and scale. The average cost of production may be U-shaped – falling until a certain level of production is reached, but rising thereafter (Houlberg, 2010; Boyne, 1995). Organisational and management theorists have long associated larger public and private organisations with increased specialisation, but equally with increased formalisation of behaviour, with more hierarchical structures, and with more elaborate administrative arrangements to communicate and co-ordinate work (see for example Mintzberg, 1983). More specifically, in the context of local government, it has been argued that larger local authorities tend to undertake more activities through direct labour and can be constrained by restrictive work practices. On the other hand, smaller local authorities can have more flexibility around work practices and can be more cost-conscious as they tend to outsource more services (Bish, 2001; Allan, 2003).

As well as the potential diseconomies of scale, territorial reforms and mergers also involve one-off transitional costs, such as ensuring compatibility of software and communications systems, time expended aligning local bye-laws and policies, and opportunity costs that arise from diverting personnel and resources from core service responsibilities to manage the transition (Fox and Gurley, 2006; Andrews and Boyne, 2012; Kuhlmann and Wollmann, 2011). Territorial reform can also lead to last-minute over-spending by 'old' local authorities before they are closed down (Blom-Hansen, 2010).

A further complication in the debate over size and costs arises from the fact that, in contrast to most public and indeed private organisations, local authorities are multi-functional bodies providing a highly diverse range of different services. This is important insofar as

21

economies of scale usually relate to the nature of production processes. Thus, the optimal size of delivery organisations varies depending on the service concerned, each of which has its own production characteristics (Houlberg, 2010; Dollery and Fleming, 2005). As different activities are likely to possess different scale characteristics, no single authority (large or small) is likely to be of the optimal size to produce all of them efficiently. Research suggests a broad distinction between labour-intensive and capital-intensive services (see for example Houlberg, 2010; Dollery and Fleming, 2005; Fox et al., 2006) with the latter offering some potential for economies of scale, but the former tending to generate few scale economies and being more prone to diseconomies of scale.

Dowding et al. (1994) in a review of some 200 studies, suggest that while the evidence is not irrefutable that smaller is more efficient, most research suggests that larger local authorities are associated with higher spending per capita, and that more fragmented smaller local authorities generally have lower levels of expenditure per capita. There is also marginal support for the proposition that citizen satisfaction with local services tends to be higher in smaller local authorities. However the results are mixed and there are difficulties drawing general conclusions about the benefits of either larger or smaller structures.

Byrnes and Dollery (2002) review 34 different studies into the relationship between local authority size and the cost of service delivery in several countries, and note that "overall, 29% of the research papers find evidence of U-shaped cost curves, 39% find no statistical relationship between per capita expenditure and size, 8% find evidence of economies of scale, and 24% find diseconomies of scale. From this evidence alone we can conclude that there is a great deal of uncertainty about whether economies of scale exist in local government service provision" (2002:393-394). A number of assessments on the topic are cited by Boyne (1995), which also suggest a difficulty in drawing conclusions that larger local authorities on the whole perform better than smaller authorities, or vice versa.

Reviewing this debate in 21 different European countries, the European Committee on Local and Regional Democracy (CDLR, 2001) is also cautious about economies of scale, and finds that larger local authorities are not necessarily more or less efficient than smaller local authorities. The CDLR report suggests costs can be higher in the very smallest local authorities, lower in medium-sized local authorities but often rise again in local authorities covering more than 40,000 inhabitants.

In terms of research into this area in Ireland, Callanan *et al.,* (2014) examined available data over a number of years on local authority expenditure and service standards to see if a statistical relationship could be established between these variables and local authority scale (as measured by population size, organisation size or volume of activity). The research found very limited evidence of correlations between local authority size on the one hand and costs and indicators of service standards on the other. Where relationships were found, the research suggested some surprising, even counter-intuitive findings, at least as far as those advocating larger local authorities might be concerned. For example, the data suggested that larger local authorities have greater difficulties with staff absenteeism and tend to have higher per capita costs in areas such as housing maintenance than do smaller local authorities. On the other hand, the results suggested that larger local authorities tend to spend proportionately less on IT overheads than smaller local authorities. These areas were exceptions however to the main findings which suggested a weak link between local authority size on the one hand, and expenditure and service standards on the other.

It seems that size is not really that important after all. Once one moves beyond populations of around 30,000-40,000, factors other than size are likely to have a far greater influence on local government costs and efficiency. Some of the most commonly cited in the literature (see for example CDLR, 1995 and 2001; Travers *et al.,* 1993) are:

- Political choices and local preferences in terms of service levels, discretionary services provided;
- Demands arising from local socio-economic characteristics (for example wealth and revenue base, degree of commercial development, rates of poverty);
- Demographic characteristics of the area (population density, age structure and dependency ratio, number of seasonal residents/ commuters);
- Local topography (geographical and physical conditions, urban/ rural area, coastal/ mountainous area, etc.);
- Management decisions and processes.

Research suggests that these factors, rather than size per se, are likely to have a greater effect on costs and efficiency.

Conclusion

For decades the dominant political position has been to avoid (or at least engage in only minimal) tampering with the territorial structures of local government. While local government has been subjected to extensive reform, it has generally been in the context of relative stability of territorial structures. However, territorial reform seems to have moved from being a 'closed' issue to a topic of legitimate debate in the period since 2009, with a number of different proposals for reconfiguring and amalgamating local authority structures seemingly gaining traction. Significant changes to sub-county and regional structures were introduced in 2014, but these have largely respected traditional county boundaries.

The impetus for the increasing interest in territorial reform has primarily come from the deficit in public finances, and the rather intuitive assumption that reducing the number of local authorities and creating a smaller number of larger local authorities will yield savings from economies of scale. As noted above, hard evidence to support such assumptions is less than conclusive. Economies of scale are arguably a more important consideration for single-purpose service providers (whether public or private) than they are for multi-functional bodies providing a range of services with different scale effects. Savings in some service areas are likely to be offset by costs (both ongoing and transitional) in others[9].

---

[9] By the same token, it is worth noting that it is by no means certain that the equally common assumption that smaller local authorities are inherently more 'democratic' than larger local authorities holds true either – again this is an area subject to extensive research (see for example Mouritzen,1989 and 2010; Houlberg, 2010; Lassen-Dreyer and Serritzlew, 2011; Swianiewicz, 2010; Lyons and Lowery, 1989; Newton, 1982).

CHAPTER 3
THE CHANGING ROLE OF CITY ADMINISTRATION IN AN INCREASINGLY URBANISED WORLD

Lorna Maxwell

Introduction

In 2010 for the first time over half of the world's population were living in metropolitan areas, and the UN predicts that as soon as 2020 this figure will grow to two thirds. The economic dynamics of this are that cities, while accounting for just 2% of the world's land surface, account for over 80% of global economic output (UN, 2010). Globalisation has led to an increase in the proportion of goods and services that are internationally traded from 19% in 1990 to 29% in 2008 – an increase of over 50% (World Bank, 2011).

The past two decades have seen lower-income metro areas in the global East and South 'close the gap' with higher income metros in Europe and the United States. The global economic and financial crisis only accelerated the shift in growth toward metros in those rising regions of the world (Berube *et al.*, 2010). Cities are emerging as drivers of national economies, but perhaps more importantly they are demonstrating a higher GDP per capita than their national average, higher labour productivity levels and faster growth rates than their national counterparts (OECD, 2006b). Cities are moving to centre stage in global economic growth trends and are competing with other cities internationally as drivers of economic and social development.

So what are the key characteristics of a city that is supporting this growth? In 2006 the OECD presented successful cities as ones that attract talented young highly-skilled workers; are centres of innovation and entrepreneurship; and are competitive locations for global and regional headquarters (OECD, 2006b). Collectively, these factors boost labour productivity, cited by the OECD as the primary factor in determining urban performance. In 2009 Ireland's National Competitiveness Council identified four cornerstones of urban performance:

- Enterprise;
- Connectivity;
- Sustainability;

• Attractiveness and Inclusiveness.

The report described an *enterprising* city as being characterised by a sectoral mix of firms that are weighted towards high value industries, the availability of a skilled workforce and competitive costs of doing business. It emphasised the importance of *connectivity* with physical and electronic infrastructure to facilitate the daily demands of trade and business and where goods, services and people can be moved quickly and efficiently. The provision of a *sustainable* urban environment is necessary to provide enhanced quality of life, maximise land use potential, attract overseas talent and tourists and reduce negative environmental costs. And finally a city that is *attractive and inclusive* where social cohesion ensures all members of society are active participants, where crime is reduced and there are vibrant recreational, entertainment, cultural and sporting infrastructures:

> Cities play an increasingly crucial role in the development of national competitiveness in modern knowledge-based economies.... they improve the economic performance of their country. However, the corollary is that, without proper management, cities can lower national economic growth rates (NCC, 2009:4).

Collectively, these represent a tremendous challenge for any city to get right and to provide a consistency that reassures the people who live, work, visit and do business there. To meet these challenges city administrations internationally are transforming their policies, services and programmes, to achieve innovative outcomes so that productivity, competitiveness and quality of life are increased while expressing a unique identity that distinguishes the city internationally and develops a sense of pride in its citizens:

> The challenge in achieving an even spread of investment [across Ireland] is intensified as the sophistication of investments increase. They require a concentration of highly qualified and educated workers, supporting infrastructure and high-level business services. Frequently, competition for

foreign direct investment comes not from other countries but from city regions with populations in excess of one million people. Dublin is the only recognised city region in Ireland that meets this criteria (IDA, 2008:3).

Dublin as an Internationally Competitive City

Though Ireland's only city of international scale, Dublin is a small city region in any global comparison, ranking 77th out of 78 cities based on population in the OECD territorial review on cities (OECD, 2006b). Dublin is a key driver of the Irish economy, accommodating 28% of the national population and producing almost half of the country's GDP. With a projected population increase of 16% that will increase Dublin's population to 1.5 million people by 2022, there will continue to be pressure on the delivery of infrastructure and services to underpin this growth and support and Dublin's role as Ireland's principal employment, business, and knowledge hub. The National Competitiveness Council expressed this urban resource dilemma quite explicitly:

> It is critical that both national and regional policies support the development of Dublin and of our other main cities and that nationally we work to ensure that the development of our cities is fully understood as being in the national interest. The challenge is not the redistribution of resources between Dublin and the rest of the country but rather of enhancing the competitive advantages of Dublin and other major urban centres as drivers of overall national prosperity and contributors to social cohesion and well-being (NCC, 2009:1).

So how does city governance address these challenges of international competitiveness in an increasingly global and urban economy to support economic growth and social cohesion, all in the context of shrinking public resources? Again quoting from the National Competitiveness Council:

In response to globalisation, many city authorities across the world are shifting their governance from a managerial approach, which is primarily concerned with effective provision of services, to one of entrepreneurialism. In this system, policymakers from different administrative institutions work in partnership with each other and a variety of public and private stakeholders to develop the city, which in turn enhances its business environment, the quality of life enjoyed by citizens and the experience of visitors. A growing emphasis on competitiveness by Irish city authorities is welcome and should continue to be nurtured (NCC, 2009:8).

As the providers of many of the city's operating systems, infrastructure and quality of life determinants, the adaptability of the local authority is centre stage in the city's ability to function and respond to these pressures. It must establish the capacity to develop innovative and adaptive systems which facilitate the development of collaborative city leadership that manages the city's identity internationally; leads in the formation of innovation, business and knowledge networks; and develops new partnership and business models to advance smart city solutions to the significant infrastructural and capacity challenges all cities face. Local authorities have a long-standing tradition of supporting economic growth (examples of which are set out below) and they are best placed to lead in the development of these new areas of expertise.

Examples of economic development activity of local authorities:

- Provision of infrastructure and managing service delivery;
- City/ County Development Plans;
- Urban Regeneration Initiatives (e.g. Integrated Area Plans; Ballymun Regeneration; RAPID Programmes);
- Land disposal and acquisition;
- Derelict site levies;
- Development of Enterprise Centres;
- Development levies to fund infrastructure;
- Maintaining competitive business rates;

- City/County Development Boards and the Offices of Community and Enterprise;
- Business Improvement Districts;
- Local Enterprise Offices (LEOs);
- Local Economic and Community Plans.

An example of this entrepreneurial mind-set is evidenced in the development of Grange Castle Business Park by South Dublin County Council attracting a significant cluster of FDI companies and leading to employment creation for about 2,000 workers. The Smart City projects between IBM and the four Dublin local authorities exemplifies the development of innovative new partnership models between local government and the private sector to share high value analysis and expertise on service delivery, research development and technology capacity, a unique opportunity in a time of resource constraint and recruitment embargoes. Opening up the region's public information particularly on service delivery and systems data is also at the heart of the *Dublinked* and the Fingal Open Data initiatives. 'Big Data' analytics is of significant economic value in terms of efficiency gains, innovation and business creation opportunities, while also supporting an ethos of open government where transparency, collaboration and engagement on complex issues becomes valued for the better outcomes generated.

Creative Dublin Alliance
The establishment of the economic development function and a growing economic agenda at corporate and strategic level for the Dublin local authorities has led to a growing focus on managing these external relations and building strategic networks and alliances across the key players in the city region. A framework for these networks was formalised with the creation of the Creative Dublin Alliance (CDA), which was a high level leadership network across the Dublin local authorities and other key government bodies; the universities and research institutions in the region; and the business /industry sector. This new approach was taken to build on the national policy framework set out in Building Ireland's Smart Economy, the National Framework for Economic Renewal launched in 2008, with a particular focus on creating 'The Innovation Island'. The triple helix model is used at a micro level to build innovation systems between industry, research

and government players. The Creative Dublin Alliance[10] was established to build a leadership alliance between government, research institutions and business at the city region level to drive the development of Dublin as a knowledge and innovation hub that could compete internationally for investment and business.

> By building alliances across business, third level institutions and local government, the potential for developing a coherent and visible leadership that has the support of these sectors is maximised. If effective, it will increase levels of trust, confidence and openness for change and place the City Region in a position to maximise the potential for innovation and collaboration (Dublin Local Authorities, 2009:17).

Its first task was the preparation of the Economic Action Plan for the Dublin Region. Led by the four Dublin local authorities, this set the framework for activity under three core pillars:

• Building Leadership;
• Developing a Vibrant Place;
• Attracting, Nurturing and Retaining Talent.

With a new focused leadership structure emerging for the Dublin region through the CDA, a coherent framework shaping activity in the Economic Action Plan, and a growing resource in the economic functions in the local authorities, new business models and partnerships were entered into, typified by the growing number of Smart City partnerships across the region addressing infrastructural challenges and sustainability issues. The Green Way was an example of the local authorities, university and local business chambers working together to support and accelerate the development of a cleantech cluster in Dublin. The cleantech sector is recognised globally as a significant growth industry with a number of centres of excellence emerging in cities across the world, as building sustainable cities becomes a critical challenge in our increasingly urbanised world.

---

[10] The Creative Dublin Alliance was wound down prior to the publication of this volume.

The Green Way[11] has been formed in order to drive our productivity and innovation using the cluster's 'triple helix' of competencies in the areas of Industry capability, Academic research, development and innovation (RD&I), and Government engagement to develop, promote and attract businesses in the cleantech sector and to stimulate job creation. Within The Green Way, Irish cleantech companies benefit from access to cleantech R&D capabilities provided by the academic institutions, access to potential procurers of cleantech products and services, as well as access to test beds and a talent pool provided by all cluster members. (The Green Way, 2011:3).

The annual Innovation Dublin programme showcased innovation across the region's researchers, entrepreneurs, innovators and creative thinkers to promote and celebrate Dublin's innovation and entrepreneurial accomplishments locally and internationally, creating new business opportunities for SMEs particularly in the Dublin region and building innovation networks at the city scale.

This growing economic focus has also led to a deeper understanding of the nature of agglomeration economics, the dynamics of both sectoral clusters and spatial economic corridors, and in particular the importance of the spatial planning and facilitation role of a city administration in supporting and developing such clusters. A co-ordinated effort across the four Dublin local authorities was led during the most recent reviews of the city and county development plans to agree three economic corridors, identified through an economic analysis of existing land use and business activity potential, as well as agreed common criteria in assessing the economic impact of a potential development.

In 2012, the Creative Dublin Alliance launched a roadmap to developing the Dublin Brand. As the roadmap states, "a dynamic and innovative Dublin brand that captures the region's unique qualities and is well managed and communicated will enhance Dublin's attractiveness as a global centre for international investment, trade,

---

[11] See chapter 11 for more detail on The Green Way.

tourism, and talent" (Creative Dublin Alliance, 2012:vi). Increased pressures on budgets and resources make it a necessity for all those involved in the development, positioning and marketing of Dublin to better collaborate and co-ordinate on this work. The roadmap prioritises the development of innovative approaches to engage citizens, a transparent governance structure, co-ordinated and integrated communications strategies and international marketing campaigns and a target-driven approach to benchmark Dublin's performance over time, building measurable 'brand value'.

A city brand is a relatively recent concept but there are many examples of successful city brand management strategies, such as New York, London, Amsterdam, Barcelona, all of which are firstly shaped by the active involvement and direction of the city administration, and secondly by a partnership model across the city's key players. This open collaborative approach is important as a good city brand will achieve beyond just tourism outcomes and could lead to better performance for the city in the attraction of investment, talent and business. Dublin's performance in attracting investment and business is monitored in many international benchmarking reports, alongside many other international cities and this is the chief measure of the brand value.

Conclusion

Recent policy documents on local government reform such as *Putting People First* (2012) highlight an increasing role for local government in local economic development, job creation and enterprise support. While the role of local government in Ireland is narrow by international comparison, local authorities are 'invested with wide and flexible powers to engage in economic activity and to further the development of their areas' under the Local Government (Planning & Development) Act 1963. Furthermore the power of general competence set out in the Local Government Act 2001 means a local authority can carry out any action or measure it deems will promote the interests of the local community through the social, economic, environmental, recreational, cultural, community, or general development of the local authority area or of the local authority, once the action would not prejudice or duplicate the statutory functions of another public body.

The devolution of responsibility for service provision to the local authority, and their remit to properly address local issues is confining.

However, the existing legal framework set out above, together with an increasing frequency of service level agreements between government agencies and departments, and an increasing competency in developing new business models and partnerships with the private and civic sectors (including transparent performance indicators), does provide sufficient basis for the development of the central co-ordination role for the local authority, whether this be in a rural or urban area.

Given the increasing and accelerating rate of urbanisation globally; the increased competition faced by city regions for international investment, trade and talent, the leadership and capacity of the city authority increasingly determines that city region's competitiveness and quality of life on offer.

CHAPTER 4
Putting People First – Accountable Oversight and Local Economic Development

Aidan Culhane

Introduction

The role of economic development in the Irish local government system has historically been weak. A lack of a coherent means of developing an economic development strategy at local level has meant that local government has been unable to act in the areas of enterprise development and industrial policy. Instead, planning, land use and other property-related instruments have been used by the local government system to facilitate economic development.

The doctrine of *ultra vires* applied to local government until 1991. A local authority had to have a specific power to act in certain areas. Otherwise it was deemed to be acting outside its competence and could be restrained by the courts. The 1991 Act, and later the 2001 Act, conferred a general competence on local authorities "to promote the community interest" and this specifically included the economic development of the area concerned. Thus, local government was permitted a far greater degree of latitude in its actions than previously. Also in the 1990s, the Better Local Government reform programme sought to radically improve local government across a range of areas, including democratic accountability and management effectiveness. This programme, which was heavily influenced by New Public Management thinking that had developed in the UK and elsewhere, aimed to develop a much more flexible and responsive style of governance.

Local Government and Economic Development

In 2012, the City and County Managers' Association (CCMA) published a report on local authority support to enterprise and business. It set out over 2000 actions "which can be seen to contribute to local development, enterprise support and economic growth". The report claimed that local government was "fundamental" to economic development. In terms of the delivery of infrastructure – roads, water, drainage, etc. – local government was the primary agency. It was also seen as either the provider or regulator of services such as waste and sanitation. These activities – though vital to economic development – were part of the core function of local government, and could not be seen solely as support for the economy. For example, the largest item identified in the CCMA report was financial support for festivals and events which, while they do provide economic opportunities (by definition short-lived), they also support the social and cultural life of the community.

Of the measures described in the report, half related to four categories of support: financial support for festivals and events; infrastructure development; provision of recreation/amenity facilities; and economic promotion. While the activities outlined showed the complexity and pervasiveness of local government action, and its undoubted contribution to economic development, they were indirect, rather than direct supports, and as such they did not show a concerted or integrated strategy to generate new economic activity or stimulate new start-ups and aid job creation.

Gorman and Cooney (2007) cite Stevenson and Lundström's (2001) description of entrepreneurship policy as measures:

- Developed to stimulate entrepreneurship;
- Aimed at the pre-start, the start-up and the post-start-up phases of the entrepreneurial process;
- Designed and delivered to address the areas of motivation, opportunity, and skills;
- With the primary objective of encouraging more people to start their own business.

This description of entrepreneurial policy would indicate that Irish local government activity in the area of economic development was focused elsewhere. As can be seen from the table below, the preponderance of activities was in areas of infrastructure provision and financial support for events. The focus was on support for existing businesses, and on acting as an agent for delivery of infrastructure. Local government's role in supporting new enterprise, and in the state's industrial policy apparatus was limited and largely confined to the micro-enterprise sector, via participation in the County Enterprise Board system. There were informal relationships between local government and the IDA and other state actors, but these were by their nature ad hoc, and not subject to any governance arrangement.

Table 4.1: Summary of Activities Undertaken by Local Authorities (CCMA, 2012b)

Description of Activity	No. of Local Authority Actions Identified
Financial support for festivals and events	465
Infrastructure development	330
Provision of recreation/ amenity facilities	227
Economic promotion including information dissemination	193
Financial incentives by local authority	182
Creating an entrepreneurial environment	141
Enterprise infrastructure	140
Establish collaborative structures focusing on economic development	128
Expenditure on recreation/ amenity facilities	109
Service enhancements/ integration within local authority	103
Policies	92
Creation of networking opportunities/structures	86
Research and innovation	71
Developing employment initiatives within community	62
Labour activation measures	53
Total	**2,382**

Economic Development, Industrial, and Regional Policy

The importance of small and medium-sized enterprises to economic development in Ireland is hard to overstate as they employ approximately 70% of the workforce. Perhaps more significant are the figures for micro-enterprises (defined as 10 employees or less) which makes up over 90% of active enterprises and over 27% of employment. Internationally, the importance of the sector is widely recognised. While Irish government policy up to the 1990s was focused mainly on foreign direct investment, it was only in the 1990s that there was a shift towards supporting entrepreneurship and the small business sector. As observed by Hanley and O'Gorman (2004), this also involved increased focus on supporting local economies as opposed to the traditional support offered on the basis of national criteria.

The importance of the SME sector is not just in the employment it sustains, it is also in its potential to create new jobs. Gorman and Cooney (2007) cite the work of Birch (1979, 1987) in the US where he claimed that over 80% of new jobs were created by small firms. They also point to the work of European researchers who highlight the importance of the SME sector for job creation. While Birch's work has been questioned i.e. the magnitude of the job creation figures for small business (See for example: Davis, Haltiwanger, and Schuh, 1996a, 1996b), research does bear out the significantly greater potential for new jobs from start-ups and small firms rather than larger concerns (See Neumark, Wall and Zhang, 2008).

Decision-making power on economic development in local areas is largely based outside of local governance structures. It is in the nature of market economies that investment decisions are made by non-governmental actors, but, governments at national and sub-national level act in a number of ways to seek to attract investment and the jobs and taxes it brings.

In Ireland, the industrial support mechanism to attract firms to locate in Ireland has been the Industrial Development Authority (IDA), while Enterprise Ireland (EI) seeks to develop and nurture promising Irish companies.

The third tier of enterprise development was via the county enterprise board structure (CEBs). Established in 1993 on foot of the Culliton Report (1992) into Irish industrial policy, these boards were set up in each county with a mandate to support micro-enterprises. Their function was to promote and assist economic development in their area of operation, which they were empowered to do via a range of loans, grants, equity investments, soft supports and development of entrepreneurialism in their areas (Government of Ireland, 1993).

The County Enterprise Boards were dissolved in 2014 and their functions transferred to Local Enterprise Offices (LEOs) in each County which are operated by the local authorities on behalf of Enterprise Ireland.

Thus, in terms of enterprise and industrial development, the state has a tripartite structure. Of these three, only the LEOs have a direct link to local government. The IDA and Enterprise Ireland's connection with local government has been via the County Development Boards, and in more recent times, the LEOs.

It is argued that most of the tools available to local government to support economic development have been in the area of real estate and property rather than in enterprise development and industrial support. Instead of making economic development a core function of local government, the state has bolted on new organisations and programmes like CEBs, EU rural development programme (LEADER) projects, partnerships etc. and then retro-engineered structures like City and County Development Boards (CDBs) to bring it together. Because parent departments and agencies are unwilling to relinquish control, the result is a lack of coherence at local level.

Industrial policy in Ireland has always had a regional focus. From the 1950s, national industrial policy sought to direct industrial investment outside the main metropolitan areas. While initially, this was based on driving investment to poorer areas, by the 1970s, and under the influence of the Buchanan report, it had begun to move towards a "growth centre" approach which continued until the early 1980s, when the focus moved to a more strategic industry approach (Meyler and Strobl, 2000). Indeed, under the IDA's strategy, one of its goals for the period 2010–2014 was "regional economic development" with the explicit target of having 50% of investment taking place outside of Dublin and Cork (IDA, 2010). The real innovation with the development of the county enterprise boards was in (a) their focus on local development (b) their specific mandate for micro-enterprise and (c) their direct linkage with local government. Board membership of CEBs included four local councillors together with a representative of the county or city manager, and the social partners.

Adshead and Quinn (1998) charted a fundamental change in attitudes to development policy in Ireland over the 1990s, a process that was to continue into the first decade of the 21st century. With regard to local government they note:

> Local government, organised at county level, now sees its authority leaking: both downwards to local activists and representatives (which were previously either ignored, or subsumed to county level of representation); and also upwards to regional agencies (which previously

either did not exist, or were co-ordinated directly by central government) (1998:212).

Thus, local government, already weak by any standards, found itself further squeezed by new entrants to the policy landscape. Area-based partnerships grew up, driven by local community activists and funded from European and other sources that the OECD described as operating in a way that "blurs familiar distinctions between public and private, national and local, and representative and participative democracy". European funding opportunities also led to the emergence of LEADER rural development programmes and consequent establishment of structures. Additionally, eight regional authorities were established in 1994 under a statutory provision to promote the co-ordination of public services, and in 1999, largely under the influence of European structural funding provisions, two regional assemblies were set up. Thus, the local government landscape changed from one based on a national/local divide with some services (e.g. health, fisheries, vocational training) provided at a regional level, to a much more complex environment.

In response to this complexity, and to improve the integration of public service delivery, in 2000 the government established City and County Development Boards (CDBs) in each of the state's 34 administrative counties. Led by local government, the boards brought together statutory agencies, the local development and community sector, and the social partners. Their remit was to formulate a strategy for their respective areas, and thus provide a more co-ordinated policy response across the multiplicity of service provision agencies. In 2008 a review of the County Development Board structure by Indecon economic consultants found that there was a need to radically improve their effectiveness. Among the criticisms voiced by participants during the review process, were that there was an unequal level of representation from different agencies, an uneven level of engagement from national-level organisations, and a lack of regard from central government for the CDBs' views on policies. The report also noted a general view that the CDBs were more effective in the area of social inclusion than in economic development, and specifically called for the establishment of an economic development subgroup of each Board. However, by 2012, the government had decided to abandon the County

Development Boards in favour of a more integrated approach within the local government structures.

At the heart of the economic development equation, and as reflected in some of the views that emerged from the Indecon study is a paradox. Economic development institutions such as the IDA and EI saw themselves as instruments of national policy, and as outside local government. The "enterprise family" of IDA, EI and the CEBs all fall within the ambit of the Department of Jobs, Enterprise and Innovation. Insofar as the national organisations take sub-national considerations into account, it is at a regional and sectoral level rather than at a local one. Thus, the CEBs, and subsequently the LEOs, are the only structure with a local focus, but their mandate is specifically to support micro-enterprise, and they have no remit for inward investment or high-growth indigenous firms.

Local Government and Economic Development

Given the weakness of the economic policy instruments available to it, local government has sought to influence economic development in its functional area by means of land use policy. Unable to use more refined methods of supporting entrepreneurship, facilitating developing businesses, or independently attracting large inward investment, the local government system placed an over-reliance on planning, in particular on zoning. Additionally, rating, a very crude property tax, furnished an additional means of signalling support for private sector enterprise. This gave rise to distortions and sometimes poor and incoherent spatial consequences.

The planning function, an explicit and unambiguous power of local government, offered a way of supporting, encouraging and facilitating economic activity within the council's functional area. Councils often saw their zoning powers as engines of economic development. Commercial development of industrial, office or retail projects offered employment and improvements to the rates base, and the provision of infrastructure enhanced the potential for development. Even residential development, which only led to short-term economic gain (in the form of development levies and construction employment) presented an opportunity for investment.

The large gain in the values of land rezoned from agricultural to classes of use with development potential, became an important impetus for political action. The subsequent corruption associated with this political action has been well documented elsewhere (see for example, the Mahon Tribunal Report, 2012). The lure of political popularity, and the prospect of promoting economic activity led to the use of rezoning, by local authorities as a tool to increase economic activity, often against official advice and frequently contrary to proper planning, and government policy.

Rates are a commercial property tax applied by local government to part-fund services and activities. In general, rating policy was seen as a pro-business signal. It was used as another tool by which local government could facilitate business interests by keeping their property taxes as low as possible. As such, it is a particularly blunt tool that can do little more than make minor differences to business running costs. As it is a tax on commercial property, it applies to all business premises almost without exception, and is therefore incapable of promoting particular industries, sectors, or even locations.

The use of these approaches by local government would point to the fact that land use, construction, and property-based instruments were seen as important linkages between local government and economic development. Taken with the provision of roads, water and other infrastructure, it could be fair to say that local government saw economic development in terms of physical infrastructure. It was a matter of physical and spatial consideration, rather than one of business development. Essentially, the role of local government was to facilitate private sector action in their area that would (a) generate investment and thus create employment, and (b) provide increased revenue via commercial rates and development levies.

A Democratic Deficit

It is worth reflecting on the distinction between "local government" as a democratically elected governance structure for a particular area, and the "local government system". Callanan and Keogan (2003) consider the Irish local government system in four ways: as an instrument of local democracy; as a provider of services; as an agent of central government; and as a local regulator.

Local government in Ireland is characterised by a divide between "reserved" functions which can only be exercised by the elected council, and "executive" functions which are exercised by the county manager. Generally speaking, matters of policy are for the elected members, while operational and day-to-day management activities are

41

the preserve of the county manager. There is very limited scope for the elected members to influence, in a significant way, the economic development agenda – other than through the planning and land use functions mentioned above. While councillors may adopt strategies and plans, the implementation and micro-level decisions will be made by the executive. The informal network of relationships between business interests, the national-level enterprise support bodies and local government is generally conducted between the management of the respective organisations.

The trend in the 1990s, and observed by Adshead and Quinn (1998) as the "move from government to governance" has been only partially arrested in the years since, leaving a rather fragmented policy landscape. More importantly however, political oversight and "ownership" of the economic development agenda has been lacking at a local level. Thus, the direction of measures to stimulate additional economic activity has been largely technocratic rather than democratic. Without either the tools or the financial resources, local government has been unable to develop a holistic strategy for economic development in its area. It has generally partnered with other agencies to undertake activities such as promoting tourism, or for business location purposes or part-funding incubator space. Indeed, it was more likely that agencies other than local authorities took the lead role in economic development actions.

Putting People First

In October 2012, the government published a comprehensive action programme for the reform of local government and local governance structures, *Putting People First* (Government of Ireland, 2012). It sets out to reform structures and to ensure that the functions of government at a local level are performed through the local government system. Specifically, it seeks to realign economic and community development functions with local government, and to streamline a confusing and unwieldy system of agencies and structures under the overall umbrella of local government.

Specifically, with regard to economic development, the document notes in regard to the role of local authorities in economic development that (2012:22):

performance would benefit from a clearer and more definite policy mandate. There is need to define a clear, coherent, and more explicit and enhanced role for local government in relation to economic development and enterprise promotion/support, both at regional and city/county level, which will complement and help deliver national policies and commitments, and also ensure avoidance of duplication or overlap with the role of other agencies.

Specifically, with regard to enterprise support, the reform programme sought to establish "Local Enterprise Offices" (LEOs) to embrace the functions of City and County Enterprise Boards and the Business Support Units of local authorities. Thus, in April of 2012, a decision was made to dissolve the 35 CEBs and transfer their functions to Enterprise Ireland.

The LEOs were established as business units in each local authority reporting to the chief executive. Under service level agreements with EI, they will provide enterprise support functions to small businesses and start-ups at a local level. In this way, a wider economic development function is given to local government, while a strong link is maintained with the state's industrial support framework, via Enterprise Ireland. The LEOs are much more integrated into local government than the CEBs had been, and should thus be more closely aligned with the objectives and strategies of the local authority. Of course, there is a risk that, as a mere business unit of a much larger organisation, they may not get the attention or resources required, but the tie-in with Enterprise Ireland and the performance of specific functions via a service level agreement is intended to mitigate this.

However, perhaps the most important instrument for economic development into the future is the new Local Economic and Community Plan (LECP) mandated by the Local Government Reform Act 2014. Local authorities are obliged to produce a LECP, *inter alia* "for the promotion of economic development in its functional area, to include the promotion of micro-enterprise, indigenous industry and foreign direct investment". The statute's clear intent is to deeply embed an economic development function into local government. It sets out a wide remit for the plans, and a detailed process of public consultation, consistency with core strategies, etc.

The subsequent guidelines on plan preparation point to a bifurcated process where the economic development element of the plan is prepared by the local authority, while the community element is dealt with by the new Local Community Development Committee (LCDC) structure. The intent of the guidelines is that both strands work from a common "socio-economic framework", and are then integrated into a single plan at adoption. A key role is accorded to the new Economic Development Strategic Policy Committees, while the overall co-ordination falls to another new structure, the Advisory Steering Group.

The guidelines also state that "it is emphasised that the LECP should not be formulated as a high-level strategy but needs to be a strongly action-focused plan", thus learning from the weaknesses of the strategies under the old County Development Board structure. In a closely circumscribed process, "Sustainable Economic Development Objectives" that are specific, measurable and time-bound are required to be produced and supported by actions. While central government has specified only indicative areas of activity, it is clear that the new plans are intended to comprehend a broad definition of economic development that includes attracting investment, supporting businesses, and increasing employment.

It is also intended that the new regional governance architecture will include a Regional Spatial and Economic Strategy (RSES) to provide "a long-term strategic planning and economic framework for the development of the region". The strategies must be in accordance with national policies and objectives, and must seek to identify regional strengths and opportunities and to augment economic performance. This must take place across a range of sectors, in particular foreign direct investment, indigenous industry, small and medium enterprises, tourism, agriculture and forestry. The strategies must also seek to enhance regional innovation capacity and identify the "regional attributes that are essential to enhancing regional economic performance" (Local Government Reform Act, 2014). The spatial element of the plan is prepared having regard to the economic plan, and deals with the location of development (housing, industrial, other commercial, and retail), the transport, linkages, provision of social infrastructure, landscape and environmental considerations.

Added to the institutional complexity of the preparation of the LECPs is the requirement to be consistent with the Regional Planning Guidelines until their expiration, and subsequently with the new RSES structure. The synchronisation of these in the first instance is messy and the LECPs may require amendment to comply with regional strategy quite early in their lifespan. As the regional element is also dependent on the production of a successor to the National Spatial Strategy, the alignment of these strategies will require an adroit administrative response.

Conclusion
Taken altogether these changes reflect a significant upgrading of the role for local government in economic development. The local elections of June 2014 marked the commencement of the new structures. The reform process has, as its stated ambition, to realign the unwieldy structures for local community and economic development and to integrate them much more closely with the local government system. This offers the proposition for a much-enhanced system of sub-national governance in Ireland. Inevitably however, there are also many risks. Much of the complexity that exists is due to the multiplicity of agencies, and while the arrangements may be streamlined, the number of funding and oversight bodies, and mechanisms at European and national level is largely unchanged. Very significant powers are reserved for the relevant minister to make regulations governing how the new local government system will operate. There are tremendous opportunities for local councils to take on the responsibilities and opportunities that exist and to maximise the potential of their area – not least in the field of economic development. Inevitably, it is the implementation of this new system that will pose the most difficulties. For ambitious elected representatives and creative, interested management local government could be recast as a real driving force for development (in its widest sense) at a sub-national level with supportive national structures. That will take confidence and trust on all sides, and a central government willing to facilitate and assist.
Ireland is a small, relatively homogenous country. However, there is scope to maximise opportunities presented by local factors and resources. Local government is well placed to co-ordinate activities to support, and draw together, the necessary expertise to ensure that the potential is maximised, and to enable and support investment and enterprise. For the first time, local democratic structures and elected representatives are in a position to lead.

CHAPTER 5
LOCAL TAXATION REFORM

Patrick King and Karl Deeter[12]

Overview

This chapter assumes the purpose of property tax – as per the *Joint EU/IMF Programme of Financial Support for Ireland* – is for government to "establish a sound basis for sub-national finances through a new residential-property based site value tax". On that basis, the property tax should relate to the amount of revenue needed to support local authority expenditure. The analysis of the revenue needs and tax base should therefore be specific to individual local authorities.

This chapter sets out the tax base options which could have informed a comprehensive public policy discourse on the issue. It then proposes and analyses a model of replacing government funding of local authorities through the General Purpose Grant with a Local Property Tax using a tax base of site size. It examines the replacement of a national funding system of local authority costs, with one based on locally raised revenue. Having approached the revenue needs of each local authority, the paper concludes by setting out tax rates based on the model proposed. The key components are firstly to use a tax based on land rather than on buildings and secondly to link the tax to the budget of the locality in which it is raised.

This chapter aims to highlight the many policy issues that were ignored by government and opposition alike.

Modern Context

The first Commission on Taxation (1985) and the Barrington Report on local government reform (1991) highlighted a need for local taxation if local government was to be given real discretionary powers. Despite this, little policy development occurred on local taxation until, as part of its commitment in the Joint EU/IMF Programme of Financial Support

[12] We would like to thank Fred Harrison (property tax economist), Donal de Buitleir (PublicPolicy.ie), Constantin Gurdgiev (TCD), Fingal County Council, Frank Quinn (SCD), Tom Dunne (DIT Bolton Street), James Pike (Architect OPM), Emer O'Suchru (Smart Taxes), Peter Stafford (SCS), Bruce McCormack (DECLG), Greg Bryan (Dublin City Council), Dublin Economics Workshop, and several others who wish not to be named.

for Ireland, the Government introduced a property tax that would be used to fund local government. In the lead-up to Budget 2012, the Local Government (Household Charge) Act 2011 introduced a household 'levy' on all homeowners, with some exceptions. While a levy system was used initially due to its ease of introduction, an Inter-Departmental Group on Property Tax was established to design an equitable property tax system for the longer term.

The subsequent political and media attention was anything but constructive. The report of the Inter-Departmental Group on Property Tax (Thornhill Report) was not published until after Budget 2013[13]. It revealed differences of opinion but did not probe different designs to any depth. It came down clearly on the side of a residential property tax rather than a site value tax.

Even the academic and policy debate was limited in contrast to other policy issues of the day. The central academic contributions came from Collins and Larragy (2011) and Lyons (2012) with the present authors' original work (Deeter and King, 2012) further expanding the design options that were subject to discussion ahead of the Budget 2013 decision.

Historical Context

Historically, tax on immovable property was 'the tax'. This changed in 1799 when William Pitt the younger introduced Britain's 'Income Tax' which was originally designed as a temporary measure to offset losses in indirect taxation[14].

The revenue was required to purchase weapons for the Napoleonic wars. The introduction of this tax was hugely unpopular[15] and was

---

[13] Fianna Fáil Press Release, 27/08/12, "FF Calls for Immediate Publication of Thornhill Report on Property Taxes".

[14] This was part pragmatism, Pitt needed a tax that could pass through the House of Lords who at the time were the more senior of two houses was made up of large land owners who would not back a site related tax (Lords Temporal or 'Peers' were monarch appointed, while 'Spiritual Lords' were Church appointed – the church was also a significant land holder). See here for notes http://www.tcd.ie/iiis/HNAG/Papers/Income%20Tax.pdf

[15] The tax was repealed, reintroduced and repealed again by Henry Addington between 1803 and 1816; Sir Robert Peel brought it back in 1842 for three years. In the 1874 elections both Gladstone and Disraeli (who were usually opposed to anything the other supported) both promised to repeal income tax. Disraeli won and did not fulfil his election promise. Gladstone's 1853 budget speech is notable for its review of the place in

subsequently repealed by Pitt's successor. Income tax came and went several times from then on before becoming a permanent fixture in the mid-1800s. Income tax did include income from land, but it did not tax the land itself meaning it kept the status quo of having no carry cost for land ownership.

In Ireland, there had been a system of rates which was abolished by Jack Lynch's Fianna Fáil Government in 1977. It was part of a populist manifesto[16] to end both property tax and motor tax but while the plan had the desired outcome of luring voters, in practice it eroded the tax base. The subsequent decline in the economy resulted in a move to extract the lost revenue from the PAYE system. Nonetheless, the abolition of these two tax revenue streams led to the highest level of reduction in taxes as a proportion of tax revenue from 1965 to 2010 in the OECD, see Table 5.1 below.

Table 5.1: Reduction in Taxes from 1965-2010

	1965	2010	% Change
Ireland	15.1	5.6	-9.6
Greece	9.7	3.2	-6.5
New Zealand	11.5	6.8	-4.8
Denmark	8.0	4.0	-4.0
Germany	5.8	2.3	-3.5
United States	15.9	12.8	-3.1
Canada	14.3	11.5	-2.7
Austria	4.0	1.3	-2.7
United Kingdom	14.5	12.1	-2.5
Portugal	5.0	3.7	-1.3
Spain	6.4	6.4	0.0
Sweden	1.8	2.4	0.6
Luxembourg	6.2	7.2	1.0
Japan	8.1	9.7	1.7
France	4.3	8.5	4.2
OECD average	7.9	5.4	-2.4

Designing a Property Tax
In designing a new property tax Ireland had the advantage of having had previous experience of property tax without being restricted by an

---

society and history that income tax held. It is worth noting that 'repealing income tax' was an election wagon in every term from 1853 to 1874.

[16] A copy of the actual advertised version is here http://irishelectionliterature.files. wordpress.com/2010/10/lynchbig77b.jpg

existing system. This offered a real opportunity for exploration of and debate on all possible options of property tax design and interrogation of the advantages and disadvantages of each.

In designing a property tax, there are several aspects which are political decisions and should be understood as such. One possibility is to base the tax on a consideration of what those who are to pay the tax will accept:

$$Tax\ Rate * Tax\ Base = Tax\ Revenue$$

An alternative approach would be to assess, similarly to a regulator, the revenue required to run the services for which the taxes are being collected. In this case, the tax rate is the result:

$$Revenue\ Required\ /\ Tax\ Base = Tax\ Rate$$

In what follows, we first assess the options for setting the tax base. We then assess the revenue requirements before finally analysing the outcome from the proposed model.

Tax Base Options for a Property Tax
Defining the basis for property tax starts with whether the primary part of assessment is the constructed property (i.e. the home) or the site (i.e. the land). Following that, it is necessary to determine the method of assessment – whether on a value basis (i.e. market value) or a size basis (i.e. total size). As Figure 5.1 shows, this provides the options for four possible approaches: property value, square footage, site value, and site size.

Property Value
A common basis for determination of property tax is property value. A market value, determined either through a central valuation office or by the homeowner (with or without professional assistance), is used as the base and a rate is then assessed against it to determine the property tax liability due for that home.

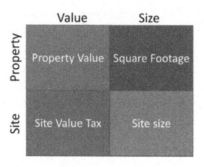

Figure 5.1: Options for Approaches to Taxation.

Table 5.2: Ranges of Property Values in England.

Council Tax valuation bands	Ranges of values in England
A	up to £40,000
B	over £40,000 and up to £52,000
C	over £52,000 and up to £68,000
D	over £68,000 and up to £88,000
E	over £88,000 and up to £120,000
F	over £120,000 and up to £160,000
G	over £160,000 and up to £320,000
H	over £320,000

A good example of the application of this approach is in England, where the Council Tax is the main source of locally-raised income for many local authorities. The Valuation Office Agency in England assesses the properties in each district area and assigns each property to one of eight valuation bands: A to H (see Table 5.2). The banding has the benefits of flexibility as values are best guess estimates of what the home would get on the market.

The rates for the bands are then determined by each council setting its rate for Band D homes, all other bands are determined by a set national multiplier to this figure. To calculate the council tax for a particular property a ratio is then applied. For example, a Band D property will pay an amount, and a Band H property will pay twice that.

The local calculation of rates controls for local factors that the national base does not take account of. Table 5.3 illustrates this. London has the lowest Band D rate and yet the average tax is only slightly above the country average, this is due to the higher value of homes in London. The importance of this will be highlighted later.

Table 5.3: Council Tax by Area 2011-12
(Average Band D and Average per Dwelling)

	Average Band D council tax	Average council tax per dwelling
	£	£
ENGLAND	1,439	1,196
By area of authority:		
London area	1,308	1,214
Metropolitan areas	1,399	1,000
Shire areas (b)	1,484	1,258
By region:		
North East	1,512	1,060
North West	1,469	1,088
Yorkshire and the Humber	1,406	1,048
East Midlands	1,486	1,140
West Midlands	1,416	1,114
East of England	1,480	1,293
London	1,308	1,214
South East	1,468	1,374
South West	1,500	1,272

Sources: BR and CTB forms
(a) Figures include parish precepts.
(b) Figures include unitary authorities.

Square Footage

Commenting on square footage as the basis for calculating property tax, the Commission on Taxation (2009) stated that "using floor space alone as a base for the tax would offend the principle of equity. A residential property owner who lives in or owns a 1,200 square foot house in an affluent area should pay more tax than one who lives in a similar sized house in a less affluent area".

This is an over simplification of the property tax equity debate. Whether a square footage methodology is horizontally or vertically equitable is questionable, as home choices and location decisions are not only economic decisions; they are not exclusively linked to income or wealth. For example, a family of five will require a larger house. If the term 'affluent area' is replaced with 'high priced homes' on a euro per square foot basis, the equity question is counter to the logic presented by the Commission. Those households located in or near an urban centre will pay a higher price than those in a more rural area, even if both live in the same size home. But if the work of both is in the urban area then costs of travel of the latter are higher. This example provides some support for the argument against market values as a basis for property tax.

As against the Commission's equity concerns as the basis for adopting the market value criterion for the tax, it could be argued that a number of different variables can be used in the considerations for a local tax; the equity consideration can be addressed adequately by progressive income tax.

Rather than equity referring to distribution of income, it can refer to the benefit principle (those who benefit from a good, should pay the tax for it). Linking the property tax to the cost of services circumvents the issue. It is about apportioning a liability based upon the residential land and the costs incurred. There may be some users who benefit (as in any system), but by and large it will be understood by those paying the tax that if there are local services that cost €100 and they wish to have a one hundredth of those services, they will have to pay €1. Our model follows this logic.

Site Value Tax

'Site value' refers to zoned land, whether it has been built upon or not. The focus here is on site value tax (SVT) and its relationship to the full economic cost of a local authority's services; it is perhaps more correctly described as a 'site cost levy'. There is an issue about SVT and how it would apply in general, if it is only levied on developed sites[17]. Such an application would mean that the benefit of the tax, as a disincentive towards land banking, would be lost.

While in Government, the Green Party enacted legislation which introduced what was referred to as a 'windfall tax' on rezoned land[18].

This was set at 80%. Imposing a 'carry cost' on zoned land[19] creates an incentive to use the land for the designated purpose, rather than sit

---

[17] For instance, in the difference between zoned RS and zoned RA where the latter is part of a Local Area Plan but may not have been fully developed.

[18] Revenue Capital Gains Tax guidance (CGT1) Chapter 4 subsection 5 (page 13).

[19] 'Zoned' implying a classification of RS or RA status, the point being that a local area plan granting general permissions would in turn create a tax liability for owners of said

on it in the hope of gains on the basis of zoning status alone, where amplification of values are generally due to the overall economy rather than specific improvements to the property.

While authoritative voices on property tax indicate that site value tax is the 'best route', it has been pointed out (Callan, 2012) that it is not common in the majority of jurisdictions. As we have no set path (but as per the Commission on Taxation, 2009 we do have a 'best option') this should not be an issue. In many jurisdictions, it is the legacy formation of the property tax that prevails. Callan (2012) also argued that it may be 'difficult for taxpayers to understand'[20]. One could counter that if you want to apply tax in the fairest manner that one should not circumvent the fairest option in order to facilitate 'simple comprehension' considerations.

This may also imply that the general electorate lack an inherent ability to understand complex topics, when in fact a large part of our attraction to foreign direct investment is the general education levels of Irish people. Further, the Dublin City Council submission to the Interdepartmental Group on Property Tax clearly states, in chapter six, that site taxes are 'equitable and easily understood'. This would indicate that there is considerable discord amongst experts, and that there is likely a level of bias being displayed rather than evidence from empirical research as none have demonstrated that site values are 'not understood' in any jurisdiction.

It is not suggested here that a site value tax is a 'cure all' solution; its adoption creates further issues for consideration, such as in relation to establishing site borders, appeals processes for site valuations, and difficulties in applying tax banding.

Site Size
Let us now consider a 'site related tax' which uses a simple accounting method of apportionment as its basis. Through the analysis of previously uncollected data on residential zoned land throughout all of

---

lands. There are other zoning types which have a portion of residential construction such as Town Centres (TC), Rural Clusters (RC), Major Town Centres (MC), but this is marginal in comparison to the bulk of which is already built upon (RS) or able to be built upon once appropriate planning is obtained (RA).

[20] This particular point was made during a Q&A session, and was coupled with a 'lack of precedent' as the reason.

Ireland's local authority areas, we have developed a local tax base simply apportioned by size. The amount that needs to be raised from this base is determined in a similar way to how Council Tax levels in England are determined – that is calculation of the spend in the area minus funding from other sources. The analysis of the local authorities' budget is then used to determine the service charge per acre of zoned land for each of Ireland's local authorities.

The income from the current household levy system does not go directly to the local authorities from which it is raised, but into the Local Government Fund, in place of exchequer funding. Under this system, the agent for the local authority is the Department of Housing, Planning, Community and Local Government. It oversees and implements the Local Government Fund; this is not a sustainable or transparent system of local tax, linked to expenditure. Such a linkage would provide for a better understanding of the tax being raised. It would reduce the likelihood of 'location gouging' of city dwellers and rural dwellers alike by letting them know that they are engaged in a process of covering their own costs of which they are the beneficiaries.

In the German federal state of Saxony there is an 'apportionment' tax system of the type described which is used to calculate the cost of rainwater tax and is levied upon the non-permeable area of land (driveways, concrete surfaces, etc.)[21]. Under this system, the local authorities calculate the amount of impervious surface area per property and this in turn gives rise to the rainwater tax bill. From an Irish perspective it may seem extreme to 'tax rain', but if the run off caused by the lack of absorption of rain becomes a cost to the community, then it is not economically different to regular household waste, and should be charged accordingly. In the German system the tax is related to the budget of the municipality, with similar properties having different bills depending on their location. This is also the model on which the Irish property tax is based. Relating the tax to local expenditure must be a primary consideration.

Revenue Required
The argument here is that the focus should be on the costs of a local authority and the amount required to replace lost revenue by switching

---

[21] The general 'Groundkeeper tax' or 'Die Grundsteuer' has been in existence since 1938.

to local taxes, as pointed out specifically in the Commission on Taxation and The National Recovery Plan.

Local authorities are often the delivery agents for vital national services, but they also have their own local service functions (Dept. of the Taoiseach, 2008:36). The Barrington Report (1991) said that Ireland's local democratic systems had been ignored for 20 to 30 years at that point, due in part to the high level of centralisation of government. It states, "democracy rests on the dissemination throughout society of a sense of responsibility and of the opportunities to exercise it" (1991:13). Central to this is the discretionary power of the local authorities and a need to link this back to a broad based local tax. The thesis of this chapter is that local authorities should be supported by local taxes and that a site tax is the best way to achieve this.

Existing Revenue Stream

The traditional revenue streams for local authorities can be broken down into two categories, either to cover a specific service or to cover general funding requirements to replace the collective service division shortfall. As is clear from Table 5.4, there is a gap between the service expenditure and the service income – whether that is from department grants or charges paid by users. When accumulated across the service divisions of the local authorities this funding gap becomes the general funding required by it to operate the next year.

Table 5.4: Summary of Local Authority Expenditure by Division

Division Summary of Current Expenditure by Division 2011	Expenditure (€ millions)	Income (€ millions)	Gap (€ millions)
Service Division A - Housing and Building	€773.3	€683.7	-€89.6
Service Division B - Road Transportation & Safety	€878.5	€540.9	-€337.6
Service Division C - Water Services	€709.8	€261.6	-€448.2
Service Division D - Development Management	€282.9	€59.3	-€223.6
Service Division E - Environmental Services	€748.8	€230.1	-€518.7
Service Division F - Recreation and Amenity	€383.8	€58.8	-€325.0
Service Division G - Agriculture, Education, Health & Welfare	€426.5	€395.3	-€31.3
Service Division H - Miscellaneous Services	€344.3	€145.2	-€199.0
Total	€4,547.9	€2,374.9	-€2,173.0

In 2011, just over half of funding was from specific funding (52.5%), of which Goods and Services charges raised slightly more than Government Specific Grants and Subsidies (52.5% and 47.5%, respectively). The general funding was predominately from

Commercial Rates (63.6%) followed by the General Purpose Grant (32.8%) and a minor contribution from the pension related deduction (3.6%). The funding system is characterised by the Indecon Report (2005) as "vertically imbalanced", with high levels of local expenditures being funded from general taxation.

Replacing the General Purpose Grant
As set out earlier, the Joint EU/IMF Programme of Financial Support for Ireland stated that the Government would "establish a sound basis for sub-national finances through a new residential-property based site value tax" (Department of Finance, 2010a:9). Based on the figures outlined above for 2011, direct Government funding represented two-fifths of the local authorities' income. The majority of the funding which was for the delivery of national services was paid by specific Departments through Grants and Subsidies. The medium term objective therefore is replacement of the 32.8% (in 2011) financed through the General Purpose Grant, with a Local Property Tax (that is, €713mn of the gap of €2.173bn shown in Table 5.4).

It is important to note that there is wide variation in the income ratios for each local authority, in particular in relation to the General Purpose Grant. Also motor tax is redistributed across the country. For example, Dublin City collected 15% of the motor tax in the state but only received 8% of the Local Government Fund. This redistribution is often explained as making up the difference in own resources – commercial rates – of one local authority against another. The graph below (Figure 5.2) demonstrates the redistribution is not that simple. The authors have not found a model that sufficiently explains the funding.

This opaque allocation system continued when the Household Charge and Local Property Tax (which goes towards the local government fund) were introduced. The money was actually collected by the Department of Environment, Community and Local Government (DECLG) then redistributed. It has been stated before that the "local government finance is the litmus test for central government's commitment to local government" (Callanan and Keogan, 2003:96). The absence of a replacement solution since the abolition of rates in 1977 demonstrates a reduced appetite for politically difficult propositions to solve the issue of local government funding.

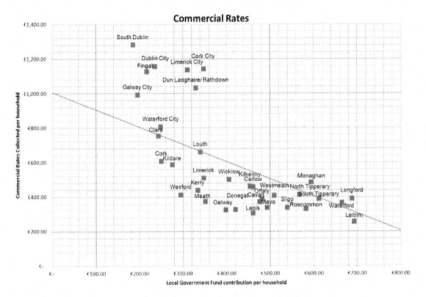

*Figure 5.2: Commercial Rates Collected vs Local Government Fund
Contribution per Household, 2011*

A Local Tax?

The Government and many Irish commentators (e.g. Convery, 2013)
have put forward the argument that those in rural local authorities do
not have access to the services of urban local authorities. They
conclude that a property tax should be higher in urban areas and
redistributed to the rural local authorities. While a logical argument,
there is no evidence to prove the value of such an approach.

According to the ESB, Ireland's dispersed population means that we
have nearly four times the electricity supply transmission and
distribution networks per capita when compared to the European
average (ESB Networks, 2017:2). In terms of roads, there is an estimated
91,000 km of regional and local roads with over 5,400 km of national
roads. This gives Ireland the second largest road network per capita in
the EU, after Sweden. The Local Government Efficiency Review Group
highlighted this point in their report. It found that 22% of local
government staffing relates to roads function (2010:70). As expected,
the level of staffing varies significantly, depending on the geography of
the specific local authority's area. In urban authorities' roads staff
represent less than 10% of total staff, compared to some rural
authorities where 46% of total staff is involved in this function. Local

authority policy is also seen to have a huge impact on this. The group cited the ability of Donegal County Council to manage twice the length of road per staff member than Mayo County Council, taking this as an indication of significant potential efficiency improvements (2010:73).

Policies and agglomeration help to explain why costs of services in remote areas are higher than in areas with higher density populations. The lower costs in higher density locations generate relative savings that can be put to use to support other services. Thus, the higher road provision per head of population in rural areas accounts for the lower level of library and other services in those areas.

From the services provided by local authorities there are several functions that generate income, either paid for by the public (individuals or business) or by other local authorities.

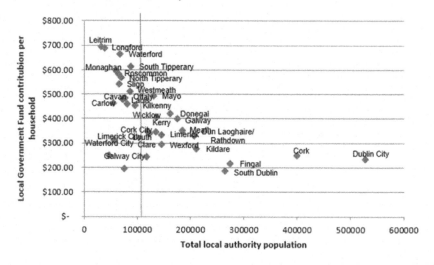

Figure 5.3: Local Authority Funding per Household, 2011

Who Pays for Inefficiency?

An objective set out in the Report of the Special Group on Public Service Numbers and Expenditure Programmes (Dept. of Finance, 2009) is for local authorities to "be self-financing in the longer term and that Exchequer support should be replaced with increased revenue generation from local sources" (Ibid.,49). An important step in achieving this objective is to analyse the traditional revenue stream.

In examining the General Purpose Grant from the Local Government Fund in more detail, it becomes clear (see Figure 5.3) that the higher level of central government subsidy on a per household basis goes to non-urban local authorities with populations below the 100,000 mark. Local authorities servicing smaller populations have significant costs.

Applying the Proposed Local Property Tax Model

Having established the revenue requirements (replacing General Purpose Grant funding) and a tax base (site size), it is left only to apply data collected to generate a tax rate per acre (or sq. meter).

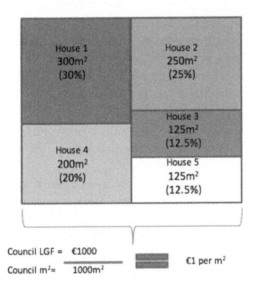

Figure 5.4: Proposed Local Property Tax Model

To recap – the proposal is that the land owners pay based on their share of land. Once the total tax base is calculated for a local authority through zoned land, the liability based on local authority expenditure (minus the areas addressed in the previous section of this paper) will be equally apportioned based on a property's local authority proportion. This method offers the opportunity to test the range of tax base options outlined at the start (market value, square footage, site value or even a simple flat household charge).

Compiling aggregated local authority specific data was completed through a process of data mining zoning documents and confirming with the local authorities by phone. The compiling of the necessary funding for local authorities was done using the Department of

Environment, Community and Local Government's Local Government Budgets[22]. For simplicity, the boroughs and town council figures were integrated into the appropriate county council.

Resulting Tax Rate

Using the methodology outlined above, the authors were able to calculate the tax rate per square meter for each local authority with the exception of Cork County, which had a level of complexity in zoning which made the calculation especially problematic (see Table 5.5).

In moving from the aggregate level (local authority perspective) to the household level, two key considerations are observed.

Firstly, the Property Registration Authority of Ireland (see Figure 5.5) has the data necessary publically available to apply an apportionment model tax with no valuations or need for further data than that which is already held. The tax would be on land occupancy alone rather than on the built portion.

Secondly, owners could easily 'self-audit' using an OSI map, Google maps (Figure 5.5) or a tape measure to ensure they are not being overcharged, with a decent degree of accuracy.

The use of these two existing tools should result in a low level of appeals which add to administration and compliance costs of a property tax. The variance is not significant enough in many cases to warrant an appeal. Appeals, as well as audits, in the first instance could be conducted by Revenue or local authority staff given the nature of the tax base. The cost of a failed first appeal should discourage frivolous appeals but keeping administrative costs down will allow those that have difficulty with the system to engage with it.

---

[22] Note that using adopted budgets of local authorities will produce different outcomes as these are often not up to date on the public websites where they are accessible.

Table 5.5 Proposed Tax Rates

	Residential zone land (hectare)	Revenue from the Local Government Fund (€ millions)	Tax per sq. m (€)
Carlow	2000	€10.8	€0.54
Cavan	2894	€16.1	€0.56
Clare	3006	€13.6	€0.45
Cork City	2543	€19.4	€0.76
Cork County		*More analysis of data required*	
Donegal	2952	€35.5	€1.20
Dublin City	4279	€57.4	€1.34
Dun Laoghaire/Rathdown	4243	€28.4	€0.67
Fingal	3968	€22.5	€0.57
Galway City	1788	€6.7	€0.37
Galway	2666	€31.1	€1.17
Kerry	3754	€25.1	€0.67
Kildare	4061	€21.8	€0.54
Kilkenny	1288	€17.8	€1.39
Laois	2747	€15.1	€0.55
Leitrim	760	€12.6	€1.66
Limerick City	1119	€8.3	€0.75
Limerick	2248	€19.4	€0.86
Longford	1799	€13.0	€0.72
Louth	2597	€17.5	€0.67
Mayo	2144	€32.6	€1.52
Meath	3922	€24.6	€0.63
Monaghan	1607	€15.0	€0.93
North Tipperary	2093	€17.6	€0.84
Offaly	2196	€14.9	€0.68
Roscommon	1958	€18.5	€0.94
Sligo	1834	€18.0	€0.98
South Dublin	3262	€18.1	€0.56
South Tipperary	2376	€23.5	€0.99
Waterford City	1137	€5.6	€0.49
Waterford	1940	€20.0	€1.03
Westmeath	1786	€18.8	€1.05
Wexford	2574	€20.2	€0.79
Wicklow	2834	€22.2	€0.78

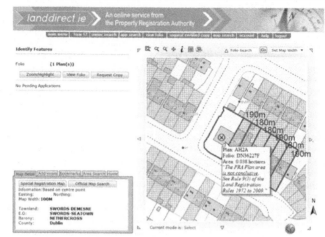

Tax liability in Fingal is €0.57 per m²

- 380sq m * €0.57 = € 216
- 190sq m * €0.57 = € 108
- 180sq m * €0.57 = € 102

Tax liability in Dun Laoghaire/Rathdown is €0.67 per m²

- 858m = €574
- 960m = €643
- 1886m = €1,263

Figure 5.5: Case Study Comparison (Image Sources: top – landdirect.ie, bottom – maps.google.ie)

These tools demonstrate the simplicity of this approach to the property tax. It means that there would be no need for a complex system taking account of the heterogeneity of different homes. It treats all zoned land (whether built upon or not) the same providing an easy to 'understand' calculation in the place of econometric models. The debate would focus on the price per metre.

Conclusion

The use of a tax system based on values holds merit, but value is a controversial issue. It can be described as contentious, difficult, and opaque. An increase in the value of a home has little impact on the owner's disposable income so assessing it straight away raises the question of the policy impact. If the property tax is designed to target those with the ability to pay, it is contradictory for there to be an exemption for private residences from capital gains tax; on selling their residence is just when the seller would have sufficient cash to pay the tax. The purpose of applying an apportionment method of taxation is to avoid the need for such arguments. Land owners pay a tax (some of which will be passed on to renters) in proportion to their share in the local authority.

Linking a tax specifically to a local authority, which to date has not been done, creates greater incentive to pay than taxes such as the property tax or household charges have done or will do. People will know they are contributing directly to their own area (not necessarily the case with the household charge)[23], and they will have no argument on valuations, or need for them – they need only a tape measure. Thus many of the issues which have caused so much difficulty to date are overcome. Moreover, there is no – in effect – punishment for a household that happens to live in a high-valued house.

Sites vary in size, and that is reflected in the market price. Two terraced houses with significantly different back yards will attract different prices assuming all other aspects of the properties are comparable. Taxing the quantum of land may be seen as crude, but it is not without precedent and it is easily understood. Making it local authority specific avoids gouging and by nature it is also a dynamic tax which aligns the interests of taxer and payer alike. For example, if

---

[23] While it is earmarked for local authorities, it is not done so with guaranteed proportionality.

people know that a waste treatment plant will be a revenue source for them and reduce their property tax they may view it differently than the standard response of 'not in my backyard'.

A major issue for municipalities the world over is what to do when values fall rapidly, and the tax take is consequently reduced while costs remain high. In many cases this can mean bankruptcy[24].

Unlike market value taxes (at least the type described to date that uses a levy approach) or the regular Site Value Tax, an apportionment model is dynamic as it is linked to costs. If costs fall so does the liability per metre – something which many councils would likely try hard to bring down and certainly something which councillors would campaign upon.

There are a few Irish local authorities that, due to what can perhaps best be classified as structural issues, would need continued general purpose subsidy until such time as the structural issues are addressed. The clearest example of this is Leitrim County Council. In 1985, the Commission on Taxation pointed out that criteria for local taxes must be that the base is capable of yielding the revenue necessary to adequately fund the local authority. In the case of Leitrim, there is some doubt as to whether this would be possible particularly given the disparity between its tax liability and the national average. In general, the local property tax payer/ local voter would be incentivised to look for greater efficiency in their services. In the case of Leitrim, if the merger of itself with either the neighbouring county councils of Sligo or Roscommon achieved a cost saving of €10 million (which would be just under 10% of their combined gross expenditure) that would improve substantially the viability of a sustainable local government for the taxpayers there.

Applying the proposed model would allow the local authority to easily provide, as illustrated in figure 5.6, their local property taxpayers with an itemised record of how their local property tax will be used. If councillors do not fulfil their election promises they will not likely succeed in future elections. The system proposed means local government governing locally rather than having a confusing crossover where TDs are often asked for help on local authority matters.

---

[24] http://newsandinsight.thomsonreuters.com/Legal/News/2012/08_August/Factbox_ Recent_U_S_municipal_bankruptcies/

Dublin City Council Invoice

Charles Cook
48 Meadow Court
Dublin 7

Date	01/01/13

Folio Reference	Ca/1090/fa
PPNS	6797104D

Cost per Hectare	€13,412.71
Site Size	175

Total Cost	€234.72

Breakdown of your local property tax's usage by Dublin City Council	m2 Cost Apportionment	Cost €
Housing & Building	0.177929	€31.14
Roads, Transport & Safety	0.132156	€23.13
Water Services*	0.190404	€33.32
Development Management	0.083314	€14.58
Environmental Protection	0.424439	€74.28
Recreation & Amenity	0.256614	€44.91
Agriculture, Education, Health & Welfare	0.010192	€1.78
Miscellaneous	0.066221	€11.59
Total Cost for the year		€234.72

*will be removed when water charges start

Figure 5.6: Sample Invoice

CHAPTER 6
VACANT LAND TAX: SOME POTENTIAL BENEFITS

Kieran Rose

> *This is an issue of 'behavioural economics'; A price causing a behavioural change – basic economics"*[25]

Overview

Great progress has been made in addressing the long-standing problems of vacant land in Dublin's inner city in past decades, in reconstructing Dublin; areas such as Temple Bar, and the Docklands in particular have been transformed. Other areas such as Smithfield and Heuston have also experienced significant high quality development.

However, a key question for Dublin now is, how is it that after fifteen years of economic boom, when Ireland experienced growth rates in GDP averaging 6.8% over the period 1993 – 2007 (Kearns and Ruimy, 2010:54), the city centre still has considerable amounts of vacant land?

This chapter examines the background to the problem of vacant and derelict land in the inner city of Dublin. It details the proposal of Lord Mayor Oisín Quinn's task force for a vacant land levy for the inner city of Dublin. Finally, it looks at how to move from policy proposal to implementation; how to focus attention on the problem and the solution proposed; how to minimise opposition; and how to build public and political support; so that legislation can be introduced by the Minister for Finance and passed by the Oireachtas. In that sense this article is the anatomy of an ongoing campaign.

Dublin's inner city has many great assets, but it is underperforming. Many opportunities are unrealised, problems are seen by some key influencers as inevitable or intractable, and there is a mind-set of low ambition for the inner city. This article deals with one particular issue, that of vacant land and the potential of a vacant land levy. I have set out the wider issues in "Inner City Myths: The City and its Opponents" a paper I delivered to the Humanities Institute of Ireland, UCD in 2011 (unpublished). The wider issues of urbanism and Dublin are also covered extensively in *Redrawing Dublin* (2010) by Paul Kearns and Motti Ruimy.

---

[25] Dr Micheál Collins, Senior Research Officer, Nevin Economic Research Institute, personal communication.

The Destruction of Dublin

"There are 150 acres of land lying derelict in central Dublin, six times the size of Stephens Green" (McDonald, 1985:332). The problem of vacant land and derelict land in the inner city of Dublin and inner city problems more generally are long established. In his brilliant and ground-breaking *The Destruction of Dublin*, Frank McDonald states that the book "is primarily a book about the destruction of the historic city's built environment over the past twenty-five years....Most of us, having lived with the degradation on a daily basis, are now so de-sensitised that we don't even bother to make excuses anymore" (1985:5).

"The old medieval city is in ruins... every street lane and alleyway is scarred by the most appalling dereliction. And most of the damage has been done over the past thirty years by the Corporation and its devastating road plans. Scores of buildings have been demolished and dozens more are due to be knocked down .... High Street once the main street of the old city, has been transformed into an eighty-foot-wide carriageway flanked by derelict sites" (Ibid., 300).

Besides the destructive road plans, McDonald also lays the blame for this inner city malaise on the flight to the suburbs by such institutions as UCD, RTÉ, hospitals and schools. There was some opposition to these moves, in a lengthy report in 1960 the UCD move to the suburbs was strongly opposed by the Tuairim group, they warned that the move would result in "grave losses" to the college and the city itself (Tuairim, 1960).

McDonald also points out that unlike other European cities, Dublin's key decision-makers and influencers did not live in the central city area, but in the suburbs and surrounding counties (Ibid., 302). The central city area "is perceived as neither fashionable nor secure" (Ibid., 333).

Most telling from the point of view of this article is his documentation of attempts to introduce a derelict sites levy. In 1979, a special inter-departmental committee studying the inner city recommended the introduction of a progressive penal rating on derelict sites. In November 1982, a similar pledge was included in the Fine Gael and Labour joint programme for government. In March 1984, Fergus O'Brien said the matter was still 'being examined' by his department. "In effect, it was being quietly forgotten - a tribute to the power of the property lobby and its effective stranglehold on public policy" (Ibid.).

A similar scenario is set out by Peter Pearson in his book; *The Heart of Dublin: Resurgence of an Historic City* (2000) where he states that by the early 1980s the city was "at one of its lowest points". He wondered how "After centuries of civic pride now Dublin Corporation played such a destructive role in the second half of the twentieth century". He sets out how most of the western quays were demolished, while the vicinity of St Patricks Cathedral "became a wasteland". The "very spirit of the city seemed in danger of being extinguished for ever". However, by the late 1980s he sees new sources of civic pride, fostering a change in attitudes towards the city through groups such as the Dublin Civic Trust, Dublin City Business Association, Students Against the Destruction of Dublin, and initiatives such as the Dublin Crisis Conference (Pearson, 2000:11-13).

In 2000 Frank McDonald published his *Reconstruction of Dublin*, describing it as a sequel to *The Destruction of Dublin*. In it he set out how much progress had been made "Dublin is a different place; it has been reinvented". Stating that Dublin was now at "a turning point", he asked the question, "will the capital continue to sprawl", "or is there a chance, despite the mistakes made in the past, of creating a sustainable city on the European model?" (2000:7-12). However, the city did continue to sprawl despite there being significant undeveloped land in the centre. One of the objectives of this proposed vacant land levy is to reduce sprawl and the need for long-distance commuting.

Lord Mayor's Task Force Vacant Land Levy Proposal

In his acceptance speech in June 2013, the Lord Mayor of Dublin Oisín Quinn set out his intention to set up a task force to examine issues relating to a possible vacant land levy and to make a submission to the budget in this regard. A high level and representative task force was quickly established including economists, businesses, property professionals, trade unionists, planners, architects and city council officials (see Appendix 1 for membership of task force). In the previous May and June I had made presentations to the Finance, and the Economic Development, Planning and International Relations, Strategic Policy Committees on the need for such a vacant land levy, and the proposal was favourably received.

To meet the deadline for submissions to the budget, a memorandum was submitted to the Department of Finance at the end of July 2013 setting out the following:

Decision Sought

The introduction of enabling legislation to allow Dublin City Council to introduce a levy on vacant land in the inner city of Dublin[26] in order to incentivise and accelerate its development, contribute to a range of potential economic benefits including optimal productive use of city land, prevention of dereliction, encouragement of economic development and job creation, tourism, and with the sustainable benefit of encouraging new inner city housing and reduced long distance commuting.

Background

Dublin City still has considerable amounts of vacant land especially in the centre city/inner city. Many of these significant vacant sites remained undeveloped after 15 years of economic boom, when Ireland experienced growth rates in GDP averaging 6.8% over the period 1993 – 2007 (Kearns *et al.*, 2010:54). In some cases, lands had the benefit of tax incentives but still remained undeveloped. There is a need to counteract any "market disincentive" that obstructs the development of these vacant inner city sites, which are key and limited economic resources.

It is clear that the current system, whereby there is no disincentive to a landowner leaving a site vacant for many years, is not in the best interest of the city, the city economy, and the national economy. Currently, the costs of such vacant sites are borne by others and by the city in general, particularly commercial rates and Local Property Tax payers.

It should be noted that currently 50% rates are payable on vacant (rateable) commercial premises in Dublin City, providing an incentive to have them let, and a penalty for leaving them vacant. Our proposal is that a similar incentive/disincentive should apply in the case of vacant land.

The proposed vacant land levy is intended to be: pro-development, pro-investment, pro-business, pro-ratepayer, pro-employment, pro-resident, and pro-community. It would also promote the interim use of vacant development land, for example for use as a temporary public park.

---

[26] The inner city of Dublin was defined and mapped in the Dublin City Development Plan 2011 – 2017. In approximate terms, the area within the canals/circular roads.

The Lord Mayor of Dublin, Oisín Quinn, put in place a high level and representative task force to consider this submission to the budget (see Appendix 1 for membership of the task force).

Definition

Currently there are the following types of land/property in the city in terms of their financial contribution to the city:

- Commercial building that is occupied and so paying 100% rates;
- Vacant commercial building paying 50% rates;
- Vacant commercial buildings that are not capable of occupation and beneficial use in its current state pays no rates or levies of any kind. (This incentivises property owners to render their buildings unusable by removing lifts for example);
- Vacant development land pays no rates or levies of any kind;
- Housing pays Local Property Tax;
- Sites that are on the Derelict Sites Register are obliged to pay 3% of market value (currently 38 on the register in the city council area);

Lands and buildings in the third and fourth categories make no financial contribution to the city council and the services that it provides. The fact that a building that is not capable of occupation and use pays no rates is an incentive to the owners of commercial buildings to make them unusable by e.g. removing lifts, toilets etc. so that no rates are payable.

In terms of equity and fairness, one of the purposes of the proposed levy is that all property would make some financial contribution to the city. For the purposes of the levy, the proposed definition of vacant land is as follows: Vacant land zoned development land which has not been developed and does not have rateable building(s) on it.

Only lands in the inner city of Dublin as defined in the city development plan are subject to this vacant land levy. In approximate terms, the inner city is that area within the canals/circular roads.

Development Plan Challenges and Policies

The proposed vacant land levy would be a significant step forward towards addressing key challenges and policies set out in the city development plan. It recognises that considerable progress has been made in improving Dublin over recent years and improved areas include the Docklands, Temple Bar and also Smithfield, Heuston etc. However, as the city plan notes in its 'Approach to the Inner City', there are the problems of "isolated clusters", "a great sense of unevenness", and a "significant number of vacant sites in the inner city that detract from its character and coherence" (Dublin City Council, 2011:31).

Accordingly, the city plan states; "It is a central aim of the core strategy to consolidate and enhance the inner city in order to augment its crucial role at the heart of the capital city and the city region. The inner city of Dublin is the most connected destination in the country and at international level, and supports a dynamic range of economic, educational and cultural clusters, together with a growing residential population" (2011:22).

Driving Innovation, Productivity and Competitiveness
"Cities offer three overlapping benefits for people and firms – proximity, density and variety" (Athey, Glossop, Harrison, Nathan and Webber, 2007).

There is general agreement amongst economists that the density and proximity in urban areas drives productivity and innovation. Accordingly, extensive areas of, or large numbers of pockets of vacant urban land have a converse effect and are a significant drag on the city and national economic recovery (Abel et al., 2012).

It is a policy of the Dublin City development plan to "recognise that cities are crucibles of innovation and that the city centre Z5 zoned area and inner city area including the Docklands is the crucial metropolitan and national resource for innovation, promoting the proximity and diversity of uses that foster innovation" (Dublin City Council, 2011:140).

Encouraging the development of extensive inner city lands provides a significant opportunity to boost the productivity and innovation potential of the city. If we can take steps to unlock the blockages to the development of these vacant central city lands, a key limited resource; it gives us a great competitive advantage to attract highly mobile international investment. NAMA and the IDA have already identified the lack of suitable office space in Dublin City as a potential competitive disadvantage that needs to be addressed. "FDI successes have strong knock on effects economically, and this includes in leisure, retail and most significantly property. As a result the number of properties in prime locations available for future FDI expansions is starting to reduce, creating a challenge in future years", according to Barry O'Leary, CEO of the IDA in July 2013.

In their report, *Our Cities: Drivers of National Competitiveness* (2009), the National Competitiveness Council (NCC) regarding Dublin, stated that, "we should not be complacent about its position as an internationally competitive location. Its continued success is critical for the performance of the entire economy....The NCC supports the promotion of Dublin as a key driver of national competitiveness." It refers to the need for "revitalizing previously dilapidated and abandoned areas in the centre of cities" and maximizing their potential.

These extensive areas of vacant lands are potentially a great international competitive advantage for Dublin. Many of our international competitor cities have fully developed centre city areas and have no space for the expansion of uses which need/prefer to locate in centre city areas.

Major employers in the ICT sector, the finance, legal and accountancy sectors, the hotel sector, student accommodation, and third level colleges typically prefer and seek city centre locations. Appropriate development of these extensive vacant lands in Dublin would add a key element to package our attractiveness as a competitive city. For example, Squarespace, recently announced that it is to establish its EMEA headquarters in Dublin stating: "We are a Manhattan-based company with urban sensibilities. We want to be in a large, vibrant, cosmopolitan city. Dublin was the obvious choice from that perspective".

In this context, and for existing city users, these vacant lands are also a significant challenge and problem for the city. Vacant sites damage the economic potential and general attractiveness of areas, to the detriment of quality of life for residents, workers, businesses, investors, and visitors. Vacant sites are magnets for anti-social behaviour, vandalism, and illegal dumping, all of which place costs on the State and others. They are a disincentive to the maintenance and upkeep of an area in which businesses/ratepayers and residents have invested. By narrowing the rates base, the hoarding of vacant city land increases the costs of doing business. Tax and ratepayers subsidise those who hoard vacant land.

Few companies will base themselves in areas with a preponderance of vacant land – and its consequent impacts of, for example, fear of crime, potential for further deterioration - as they are competing for employees and customers. A negative cycle of under-development is put in place. Companies may invest if they feel that the vacant land levy is a strong disincentive to hoarding of vacant land; and so a positive cycle is put in place.

Benefits of a Vacant Land Levy
As already stated, because there is no disincentive currently to a landowner for leaving a site vacant for many years, and the costs of such vacancy are borne by others and the city in general, it is proposed to introduce a levy to remedy this situation. It is considered that an appropriate levy, to be payable on vacant land, would incentivise and accelerate its development, or foster its sale to those who have the interest, and access to resources, to develop it.

Such a levy would have a range of potential economic benefits. As already stated, these include: encouraging more optimal productive use of city land, preventing dereliction, encouraging economic development and job creation. The levy would also have sustainability benefits in encouraging new inner city housing and less long-distance commuting, reducing costs to business, encouraging tourism and restoring community pride in a neighbourhood.

Encouraging the optimal use of land is particularly appropriate in city areas such as Dublin where there has been and will be considerable public investment in providing services such as public transport (e.g. Luas). These vacant sites are not delivering the economic return to the public and the city for such considerable public investment.

A requirement could be put in place for the city council to keep a public vacant land register of the site location, a site map, its area, ownership etc. and also make it available on-line. It would be very useful market information for investors and developers, as well as policy makers, concerned members of the public and others. There is already a statutory requirement for local authorities to keep a Derelict Sites Register under the Derelict Sites Act, 1990.

A vacant land levy should be seen as part of a suite of revitalisation measures to be taken by the city council, government, the private, community and philanthropic sectors to continue to enhance the attractiveness and competitiveness of the city. Other initiatives include the €60 million Parnell Square Cultural Quarter; the €370 million BXD Luas line; the Jessica EU funding project; the 26% reduction in city council development levies; IDA plans for a 21st century IFSC[27] and the multi-million euro Dubline (Fáilte Ireland/Dublin City Council visitor route from College Green to Kilmainham). Temporary uses such as allotments and event spaces are being introduced on Dublin City Council owned sites, one example being the 'Granby Park' on Dominick Street

Supporting Policy and Research

The Commission on Taxation (2009) considered these issues in detail and concluded:

> We are proposing a recurrent tax on zoned development land where such land is not being developed. This will be a useful policy tool to address the hoarding of land-banks and help to ensure that land is utilised in accordance with its planning categorisation.

The Tax Strategy Group report (Department of Finance, 2010b) also set out the benefits of a land value tax as including;

- Encouraging compact city centre development;
- The most productive use of high value land;
- Those who have not developed valuable land are encouraged to do so;
- Counteracting any market disincentive to develop the land.

The All Party Oireachtas Committee on the Constitution (APOCC, 2004:87) in its 9th Progress Report on Private Property recommended the following:

> The government should devise a scheme comprising a structure of progressive charges, whereby planning authorities can secure the release of development lands where development is not being actively pursued by the owners or the development land is not being placed on the market by them.

---

[27] Nick Webb, "IDA aims to create new IFSC district", *Irish Independent*, 16th June, 2013.

In a paper on *Approaches to Land Management, Value and Betterment* (2004), the National Economic and Social Council (NESC) states that the APOCC analysis of the land market is that this market operates imperfectly. The system of land use planning leads to "a perceived shortage of development land", a signal to entrepreneurs to involve themselves in the acquisition and holding of zoned development land and "an incentive to maintain the shortage and keep values up by not developing the land until it suits their interest" (APOCC, 2004:84-5). "This implies that there may be artificial scarcities of land and land prices that may be higher than necessary".

Although we are not proposing a site value tax as such, the benefits set out for such a site value tax also apply to a vacant land levy. So for example, the NESC paper continues, "A site value tax could possibly improve land use by encouraging infill development; i.e. the development of unused or underutilised land in existing urban areas. It also acts as a penalty on derelict sites since the owners are liable for the site value tax even if the site is not generating an income. If withholding of land were to occur, a site value tax could provide an incentive to avoid this. Taken together these potentially provide an incentive for improved land use and hence would potentially support better planning" (NESC, 2004:13).

A site value tax can be expected to put downward pressure on land prices, since a buyer of land (or property) is acquiring an ongoing liability to pay the land tax as well as the asset, according to the NESC. Annual property taxes are common across OECD countries. They are typically applied to both the value of land and buildings. In Denmark there is a specific tax on land or site values. In a submission to the *Barker Review of Housing Policy* in the UK, it was argued by Muellbauer (2003), a leading British economist, that the Danish land tax improves the functioning of the land use planning system, by increasing the costs of land hoarding when land prices are high, so increasing land supply counter-cyclically.

In a May 2013 Article IV report to the UK Government, the IMF stated that "To mitigate this risk [of house price increases] and engineer a supply response, the government should consider fiscal disincentives for holding land without development" (IMF, 2013).

How a Vacant Site Levy Scheme Could Work

The amount of the levy would be a matter to be considered. Under the Derelict Sites Act, such sites are obliged to pay a levy of 3% of market value (see Appendix 2).

The primary purpose of the vacant land levy is that the land be developed or used so that it is no longer a blight on the city. The legislation could provide for a reduced/zero levy where the site has a compliant interim use such as a temporary park or playground[28]. A temporary surface car park would be excluded as this is an unsustainable use with an income that dis-incentivises its proper development.

The Local Government Business Improvement Districts Act 2006 is a precedent in that it allowed the city council by resolution to specify a part of its administrative area as a Business Improvement District and introduce inter alia a levy (see Appendix 3).

Conclusion of Memorandum submitted to the Department of Finance

To deliver on the Dublin City Development Plan and national objectives for the city, to enhance Dublin's attractiveness as an economic, business and tourist location, to achieve for the residents, workers, businesses and visitors an integrated and attractive city and to tackle the no-cost lock on vacant land currently enjoyed by landowners that is advantageous only to them, it is recommended that legislation, that would allow Dublin City Council to introduce a levy on such vacant land in the inner city, be approved.

Consideration could be given to examining and reporting on its effectiveness over a period, and as a possible model for other urban locations in the country generally.

Building Public and Political Support

Realising that the enactment of such enabling legislation would require public and political support, the Lord Mayor and the task force decided that there was a need to build wide public and political support and that public attention should be focused on the significant problem of vacant land, and the possible solution (in part at least) of a vacant land levy. It was decided to make the budget submission publicly available,

---

[28] Danielle Furfano, "Bill would help turn vacant lots into parks, gardens", *Brooklyn Daily*, 26th July 2013. Available at (http://www.brooklyndaily.com/stories/2013/13/all_vacantlandincentives_2013_08_02_by.html). Accessed 26th January, 2017.

including on the Dublin City Council and the Lord Mayor's websites (it would in any case have been available from the Department of Finance under Freedom of Information legislation).

To further drive the proposal for a levy, higher up the political agenda, it was decided that there should be significant engagement with the media. There was extensive coverage on this issue in The Irish Times through a series of high profile articles by Olivia Kelly. The photographs of vacant sites which accompanied the articles had a persuasive impact and worked well as a means to communicate the negative impact on the city of such sites.

In one article[29] Olivia Kelly wrote:

> No one gets a free ride, except owners of vacant sites. Buy a site to develop it and, if that doesn't work out, the thing to do is clear it of any structure that might attract a levy, stick up a hoarding and walk away. Then wait for the market to recover, perhaps 10 years or more. Meanwhile the city is left with an eyesore, neighbouring businesses lose footfall and potential investors are put off by the rundown appearance of the area.

In another article[30] Lord Mayor Oisín Quinn is quoted as saying "if you have people holding on to land that could be developed you are depriving the city of the potential to grow in a sustainable fashion." "In the core of the city there are sites people held on to during the boom, perhaps they were hoping the market would just keep rising. What we don't want is people who sunk money into sites during the boom holding on for another four or five years."

The possibility of a 'forced sale' of unused land was floated by the Lord Mayor; "If the levy is not paid the council can force the company owning the land into liquidation", he said. "If you don't pay your levy you get served a 21 day demand. If that debt is not paid we put in a petition to wind up the company and put in a liquidator." The liquidator will then put the site on the market".

---

[29] Olivia Kelly, "Everyone stumps up cash except land hoarders", The Irish Times, 5th August 2013.
[30] Olivia Kelly "Developers may be forced to sell vacant sites" The Irish Times, 5th August 2013.

The Office of Public Works (OPW), the organisation with responsibility for the management of state lands, came in for particular criticism particularly for its large site at Hammond Lane and beside the Luas line; described as "one of the most unsightly in the city"; and vacant for 14 years. When asked what its plans were for this site the OPW said it was being "retained for strategic purposes".

Derelict Dublin[31], a hard-hitting editorial in The Irish Times set out the background to the current problems: "It is now just over thirty years since this newspaper published a long-running series of articles under the heading, "Derelict Dublin" that documented the decay and degradation of the inner city. At the time, in 1982, it was estimated that the amount of derelict land was equivalent to six times the size of St. Stephen's Green - including highly visible sites all along the Liffey Quays".

The editorial went on to refer to the range of urban renewal incentives introduced by the then Fine Gael-Labour coalition government in 1986 and how "Dublin went on to experience its most significant urban renaissance since the late 18th century, gaining a wealth of new buildings and public spaces and, in the process, managed to reverse decades of inner city population decline".

The editorial was particularly critical of the OPW: "It is not adequate for the Office of Public Works to say that it is holding prominently located sites along the Luas line at Church Street [Hammond Lane] or at Military Road, opposite Heuston Station, for what it describes as 'strategic purposes'. The Church Street site, in particular, is in a disgraceful state, surrounded by a flimsy hoarding and full of buddleia - the tell-tale sign of urban dereliction. And since nobody knows when this site might be redeveloped, surely it would make sense for it to be used in the meantime as a temporary public park, at relatively little expense?"

In a revealing follow-up article in The Irish Times[32] it was reported, based on access to a 2009 confidential OPW document, that the OPW had 'long-term plans' for the redevelopment of the Four Courts complex including the vacant Hammond Lane site for a new legal campus. However, "the estimated cost is not included in the copy [of OPW report] seen by The Irish Times". It seems likely that this leaking

---

[31] "Derelict Dublin", *The Irish Times,* 10th August, 2013.
[32] Ruadhan Mac Cormaic "Four Courts overhaul plan sets out vision for city-centre 'legal campus'" *The Irish Times,* 29th August, 2013.

of the document was an attempt by the OPW to deflect focus on their vacant sites. What it also shows is that property owners are vulnerable to criticism about their vacant land holdings; that 'openness, transparency, and accountability' have very positive impacts; and that the media, including the social media, have a powerful role in holding property owners to account.

To be fair to the OPW, a model of good practice is their announcement that a new online property register for public buildings and land will be established by the end of March in 2014. This new web-based portal will bring together core information about state lands and buildings so that the public can see "for the first time what we own [and] where we own it" (Ibid.).

The political aspect of the proposed levy was covered by Niamh Connolly in an article[33] where she quoted a State Street bank submission to the City Council about a vacant site which adjoins its HQ in Docklands; "The undeveloped land is unsightly ... and by remaining undeveloped is a security risk to employees moving through the area. This was followed in September by another article[34] where is was stated that such a levy would be "an added burden for developers already under financial pressure" according to Construction Industry Federation (CIF) Director General Tom Parlon.

The political angle was further covered by Olivia Kelly[35] where she wrote that Minister of State for Planning Jan O'Sullivan, in a letter to the Minister for Finance, had "put her weight behind proposals for a levy on vacant development sites to end city centre land hoarding". The Minister of State was quoted as stating that, "the issue of state-owned sites that had been left vacant should also be examined, and she wanted a role in feeding into the formulation of policy in that regard. The Office of Public Works and local authorities own many prominent, unused sites". The article concluded that "Ms O'Sullivan's letter lends authority to a proposal that already has widespread support".

The property market in Dublin has begun to pick up[36].

---

[33] Niamh Connolly, "Labour seeks to tax unused land and boost development" *The Sunday Business Post*, 11th August, 2013.

[34] Niamh Connolly, "CIF attacks Labour plan for levy on vacant development sites" *The Sunday Business Post*, 8th September, 2013.

[35] Olivia Kelly, "Planning Minister Jan O'Sullivan backs mayor's proposed vacant site levy" *The Irish Times*, 19th August, 2013.

[36] Donal Buckley, "Development land prices triple in less than a year", *Sunday Business Post*, 27th October, 2013.

... and with a pick-up in demand for city centre student accommodation and offices, developers are having to compete again with investors [my emphasis] who plan to buy and sit on the land in the expectation that they may get a better return than from other types of investment.

Economist Jim Power analysed the rising house prices and the scarcity of supply in Dublin[37] and concluded that

While concerns about another bubble look pre-mature at the moment, there is always a possibility that if the market continues to gather momentum, an unsustainable market could become a possibility at some stage.

He recommended that:

For policy makers, now is the time to start thinking about measures that might prevent such an eventuality. The Lord Mayor of Dublin, Oisin Quinn recently sought the introduction of enabling legislation to allow Dublin City Council to introduce a levy in vacant land in the Inner City of Dublin in order to incentivise and accelerate the development of such land. Given that the lack of supply in Dublin is an issue that will become much more real over the coming years, this measure makes eminent sense and should be pursued as a matter of urgency.

Conclusion
In a relatively short period of time the proposal for a vacant land levy has had a number of positive impacts. For example, a steering group and a working group have been established by Dublin City Council to make progress on these issues of vacant and derelict land and buildings and related issues.

---

[37] Jim Power, "Housing strategy essential as market moves", online *Daily Business Post*, 31st October 2013.

One of the great barriers to progress in many areas is when a problem is seen as inevitable and intractable, that's the way it is (in Dublin) so don't even bother trying to change it', or too complex, so the problem is ignored/seen not to exist. As Frank McDonald suggested (see above) people become 'desensitised'. In this case, attention has been re-focussed on the problem of vacant land in the city, that it is not acceptable or inevitable, and that there is a possible straightforward (partial) solution.

Arising from my experiences of trying to achieve change across a range of areas, I have often threatened to write a book entitled, *That Will Never Work, 101 reasons given to stop or delay change.*

Laurence Bond, Head of Research in the Equality Authority, on the issue of trying to get evaluation measures introduced into organisations has summarised such reasons elegantly:

> My sense from a range of organisations is that nearly everyone seems to have a reason why doing this is not a good idea/not feasible or not whatever - often for a whole lot of different reasons. Some of these are more or less good reasons but the net effect typically seems to be that whatever is feasible is never seen as good enough and whatever is seen as good enough is never feasible - with the result that nothing much happens![38]

There is growing and wide support including from the business sectors, trade unions, elected representatives, economists and other relevant areas of expertise (as seen for example in the task force representation) to address the issue of vacant lands in the city. In a sense it has captured people's imagination, it is simple and fair, the response often has been along the lines of, 'why was this not introduced before?' However, for some interests it has caused a degree of consternation.

The Lord Mayor's Task Force continues to meet with relevant bodies such as NAMA, CIF, Property Industry Ireland and others to clarify aspects of the levy proposal, address concerns, and to build a wider consensus. One of the great benefits of setting up the task force is the bringing together of various areas of expertise such as economics,

---

[38] Personal communication.

planning, architecture, real estate, and chartered surveying, that usually exist in silos. Indeed listening to the incisive and expert (and succinct) discussions at the task force is a fascinating learning experience.

We are hopeful and determined that the vacant land levy is a measure whose time has come.

CHAPTER 7
NAMA AND THE POTENTIAL FOR LOCAL ECONOMIC DEVELOPMENT

Hilary Murphy

Introduction

The actors that contribute to local economic development range from local authorities, investors and entrepreneurs, to employers, development agencies and community enterprises. The institutional responsibility for local economic development lies with no single institution but arguably is best housed within local authorities. However, the extent to which each of the range of actor's influence local economic development is variable and determined by local conditions and the unique characteristics of localities (World Bank, 2012).

Despite these variables, there are some factors and local conditions common to enhancing the potential for local economic development across the majority of economy types, sizes and scales. These broadly relate to infrastructure, service and accessibility, economic sustainability and attractiveness. An increasing emphasis on employment creation through local economic development has been a feature of the dialogue in recent years and the role of local area partnerships in developing marketable skills, providing retraining etc. has received much attention. Attempts by local authorities to facilitate co-ordination in this regard and encourage participation, further support the case for local authorities to act as a natural institutional authority on local economic development (Ó Riordáin, 2015).

NAMA Overview

Since the creation of NAMA in late 2009 there has been broad acknowledgement that this powerful Agency will likely influence local economic development significantly at a time when many local economies are vulnerable. Little dialogue occurred then or since as to how to classify and engage with NAMA as an actor in local development. This is a contentious issue within local economic development fora.

The National Asset Management Agency was set up as an emergency solution to the Irish banking crisis. Operationally, NAMA has functioned as an asset management company by freeing the five participating institutions (Allied Irish Bank [AIB], Bank of Ireland [BOI], Anglo Irish Bank, Educational Building Society [EBS] and Irish Nationwide Building Society [INBS]) of their riskiest loans. The transferred loans were generally secured on development land and property under development and included both performing and non-performing loans. For loans to be acquired by NAMA, they had to be from one of the five participating institutions and made up of 'land and development' loans that exceeded particular thresholds. For Anglo, EBS and INBS the threshold was €0 while for AIB and BOI it was €20 million.

At the time of its establishment, NAMA was given an estimated operational timeframe of 7 to 10 years with an objective to achieve the best possible return on its managed assets for the Irish tax payer. This objective was to be realised through NAMA's powers to hold, dispose of, develop and/or enhance assets under the agency's management. NAMA 'purchased' the relevant loans at a discount from the participating institutions. The price it paid was based on the then market value of the assets, adjusted to NAMA's own determined view of the assets' long-term economic value.

Inevitably, in the majority of instances, the long-term economic value was significantly less than the outstanding loan held by the borrower. The total book value (the value at which an asset is carried on a balance sheet) of the loans managed by NAMA is in the region of €80 billion, but NAMA did not pay anything near this figure in acquiring the loans. At the preliminary stages of this research NAMA had acquired €72.3 billion in property loans and paid €30.5 billion in securities. NAMA's entire portfolio consists of 850 borrowers amounting to 11,000 loans on 16,000 properties. 180 of the 850 borrowers have borrowed a combined sum of €62bn. Three developers owe €8.3bn between them.

The remit of NAMA is restrictively narrow in its definition, laying out the agency's priorities as the securing of a monetary return for the tax payer as being the 'best possible return' for the public good. Appropriate as this may have been as an emergency response, it constrains NAMA's ability to engage with the issues of broader development. Those operating in the local economic development sphere have questioned if the value of NAMA to the Irish tax payer in providing a monetary return on assets is short-sighted.

Undoubtedly NAMA is, and will remain, an influential institution in matters of physical planning and local economic development throughout its lifetime. However, the manner in which NAMA 'treats' the land and development assets it manages does not oblige the organisation to participate in local economic development dialogue, contribute to planning or engage community stakeholders in its decision making processes regarding the sale of assets. A further issue is the myriad of technicalities regarding asset ownership, entitlements of privacy in the transaction making process and other associated administrative rules. On acquiring loans, NAMA does *not* assume the role of landowner and despite its authority to make decisions on finishing and/or investing in partially developed assets; neither does it act as 'developer'.

Also, it is an asset management agency, not a bank, it does not have a banking license nor does it take deposits from the public. Similarly it is not a liquidation vehicle but has been described by Government as a 'workout' vehicle with a longer term approach to borrower's assets and taking action only in the interest of commercial viability. Although not a bank, in some regards NAMA does indeed *act* like a bank in how it deals with loan details, account privacy etc.

NAMA and Local Economic Development

The powers of NAMA in influencing local economic development become clear when we examine the typical process by which it carries out its activities. There are three aspects to asset management: loan acquisition, the making of fundamental decisions concerning how best to bring the asset to an optimum marketable state and the final disposal of the asset.

The borrower of a NAMA managed loan is required to submit a detailed three-year business plan to NAMA. It is then up to NAMA experts and associated advisors to determine whether this business plan is viable and either approve, reject or refer the plan back for amendment. Business plans generally do not stray far from what the initial vision was for the asset according to the planning permission granted and/or the terms of the loan initially required. If a plan is approved, NAMA is required to closely monitor the subsequent activities of the borrower in ensuring adherence to the agreed course of action. If a plan is rejected on the basis of it being unviable, NAMA will take the necessary action in managing assets to protect the tax payer. In this case the appointment of statutory receivers is a likely route or other measures such as liquidation. In the case of a business plan being referred back to the borrower for amendment it is unclear as to what extent NAMA may advise or direct that amending process.

Business plans include all of the developer's assets and are reviewed by a board of 'non-NAMA' professionals and also an independent business plan reviewer. Individuals and groups involved in assessing business plans also have advisory powers as to how a plan may be optimised. In cases where it makes financial sense, NAMA may provide investment capital in order to enhance the possible return to the tax payer. This is generally the case where developments are close to completion and need capital to generate cash flow through rental or disposal. NAMA may also enter into partnerships and joint ventures in order to ensure the completion of a project.

Projects that no longer make financial sense are not pursued if NAMA deems them not to be commercially viable. What makes 'financial sense' is generally determined by NAMA through taking a short to medium term view. There are no final dates defined or timelines allocated for the business plan review process. However, it is in NAMA's interest, in keeping to its remit, to facilitate sales of assets as quickly as possible.

Potential of NAMA to Positively Impact Local Economic Development
In order to maximise the potential return on assets where an end use demand does not exist for a development, 'change of use' is an option which NAMA have to consider. The NAMA developments which have received the most critical attention, often due to their rapid devaluation, are generally residential, commercial or mixed use developments on urban peripheries, or land assets within urban catchments. The nature and location of these assets makes for uncertainty as to the most optimistic market value achievable under their existing designations. End use demand for typical NAMA developments is often not strong enough to secure the viability of managed assets for the purpose for which they were intended or for pursing similar type projects where they were planned.

In considering a change of use, projects which would have a social dividend i.e. schools, hospitals, community orientated developments are not given special rates as this would not meet the interests of NAMA in creating a financial return for the tax payer. So 'change of use' options are not likely to be considered in any radical sense, beyond the transfer of residential to commercial or vice versa. It has been suggested, however, that in some cases hotels and other developed buildings could be converted to nursing homes, private hospitals or similar uses as viable and financially sound changes of use.

Interestingly, and significantly from a local economic development perspective, NAMA hold sweeping powers to compulsorily purchase lands in the interest of fulfilling their objectives. This allows it to avoid, or potentially overcome, legal challenges by developers when acquiring their lands and also to acquire lands which are not associated with any of the participating banks. NAMA legislation permits the agency to compulsorily acquire land in the name of dealing with assets expeditiously and to protect or enhance the value of assets. Protecting and enhancing the value includes providing that building assets be used for the purpose which they were developed. This may allow for NAMA to compulsorily purchase land to provide for car parks, service areas and other necessary ancillary services. It also has powers to compulsorily purchase lands to provide material benefit to the use or development of assets in granting a purchaser a 'good and marketable title'.

Where the impact of NAMA on local economic development is the most tangible is where the potential for local economic development is already vulnerable. The urban centres of Dublin's north fringe are a good example of where the uncertainty surrounding the future realisation of village centre projects, (such as in Ballymun, Finglas and Coolock), is due essentially to the privacy obligations of NAMA's legislation in managing its assets in these areas. The NAMA managed developments across much of North Dublin involved the regeneration of struggling urban centres and, in some instances, the creation of new 'towns' or town centres, identifiable by planned hubs of mixed use developments local to an established community. In these instances, all other elements required for local economic development to grow, are reliant on the final outcomes of the management of these assets and on how attractive, or otherwise, the outcomes are perceived to be within the broader economic community.

Also in such areas, where the social, economic and development issues tend to be homogenous, investment by NAMA in making one particular development marketable can mean disadvantaging similar developments in the same region. Therefore, any provision of capital to enhance close to completion developments in some cases and not in others may further marginalise urban centres within the same economic catchment area.

Another obvious issue concerning NAMA's impact on local economic development potential stems from the lack of transparency of the agency's activities. When landmark developments, centres of employment, strategic land parcels, village centres etc. are reported to be under NAMA control, the variation in the outcomes of potential NAMA decisions range from complete demolition to investment and up-scaling. This variation and associated uncertainty is a deterrent to investors and dwarfs all other local economic development considerations even where they may appear attractive. There is little that can be done outside of a change to the legislation that could overcome this issue of ambiguity.

Regardless of whether NAMA relates most closely to the role of a bank, a landowner or a temporary liquidating vehicle in its interface with the development community, it is a certainty that NAMA is a public entity managing, what are technically, public land and development assets. The argument therefore for NAMA to engage actively with local authorities in matters of public interest, given the opportunities presented by public control over development decisions, is a very logical one. Although this is not an opportunity which is exploited within the existing NAMA legislation, there have been instances where the agency has engaged in some dialogue on the subject, even if somewhat reluctantly. The Annual Report of 2011 aimed to be more transparent and made reference to issues of engagement with third parties with a view to having regard for local authority land needs and the principles of sustainable development (NAMA, 2011a).

Public scepticism of NAMA's ability to create a return for the tax payer and a prevailing mistrust of political interventions in the hangover of the economic crash, contributes to the problematic status of NAMA as a faceless and silent institution. This is further aggravated by the constraints on NAMA to participate meaningfully in local economic development and planning dialogue, particularly in relation to individual loans.

There are, of course, situations in which NAMA activities are likely to give a significant boost to local economic development. This is primarily in cases where its assets are located in regions of growth and other supporting influences (such as education centres, transport links, large scale private investment etc.) combine to create an environment where NAMA can more easily achieve good market returns with a clever sale or further investment in assets.

An important question that must be posed is to what extent does NAMA's national interests and objectives, which are clear and valid, compromise the potential for local economic development as regards decisions on *individual* loans? It may be too early in the lifespan of NAMA to properly assess the balance between the agency's legislative position in carrying out its operations and its broader objectives in contributing to eventual economic recovery, but indications suggest that a conflict exists. Making highly influential decisions on individual loans without reference to local economic development considerations is unlikely to achieve long-term positive outcomes for a national sustainable economic recovery.

The research on which this chapter is based would suggest that, in the immediate term, the principle threats to local economic development by NAMA activities are predominantly around issues of transparency and engagement. The fact that stakeholders and investors must await for the outcomes of decisions on NAMA managed assets, without any engagement prior to that, has implications for local economic development potential. NAMA's remit does not facilitate a two way dialogue concerning local social, economic or environmental matters in its decision making processes. Thus planners, policy makers and local development agencies have no choice but to carry on with little regard to potential NAMA impact on plans and planning. While NAMA's processes on managing residential and commercial assets remain classified, they are ultimately de-valuing their own portfolios as local authorities remain uninformed and continue to zone and plan for growth as normal.

In terms of local economic development, despite the employment and investment opportunities of the boom years, Ireland continued to suffer social and economic problems in many marginalised communities. Such problems are considered to be of a scale disproportionate to a country whose economic performance was at the time considered one of the strongest in Europe. Arguably, this highlights the shortcomings of the spending and policy making at that time. In this regard, the fact that local economic development was not a consideration in NAMA legislation can be seen as a regrettable oversight of Government, at a time when socio-economic indicators pointed to a need for strong and inclusive local economic development interventions.

There has been much speculation as to the future of NAMA post-2020 as it concludes its asset management activities. The position of NAMA as a powerful public institution at a time of importance for aligning the management of state resources to realise local economic development potential, makes for new opportunities for it to intelligently contribute to economic recovery. NAMA is in a prime position to make strategic decisions about local economic development. Using the geographical and service attributes of local economic development areas in optimising potential, it could ultimately act as a major facilitator of local economic development by intelligently developing lands and creating a physical environment supportive of the needs of local economic development activities.

Many suggestions were gathered during the course of this research on how to optimise NAMA's powers for the benefits of local economic development. One such was regarding the practice of 'active land management'. This method of managing land assets has been practiced by the governments of Denmark and the Netherlands under similar circumstances involving institutions with remits similar to NAMA. Fundamentally, active land management involves the prioritisation of some sites for development over others. Generally, this means the prioritisation of state owned sites (or in the Irish case, NAMA managed sites) for development when the need arises over privately owned sites. This approach can enhance opportunities for bridging sites suitable for development together through the powers of pre-emptive rights. Operating in this way can also maximise the potential for the delivery of planned infrastructure and therefore provide greater potential for local economic development. Active site management goes beyond simply approving viable business plans and takes a strategic position with a strong emphasis on enhancing the prospects of publically 'owned' assets in the sole interest of the tax payer.

The adaptation of this approach for an Irish context would present problems with issues, such as those concerning competition law, in the favouring of sites based upon ownership. However as international examples show, a common characteristic of competitive and sustainable cities is a high percentage of state owned land, allowing for strategic planning unaffected by county boundaries or private interests.

Overcoming barriers to the potential for NAMA to adopt a more active approach to asset management would require a legislative amendment. The introduction of new legislation or the drafting of amendments could address the remit of NAMA in a way which would allow it to use its extensive powers more innovatively and strategically.

The influence of NAMA also presents opportunities for engaging with infrastructure providers to deliver projects at a reduced cost and potentially ahead of schedule. Many strategic infrastructure projects require the acquisition of land in order to allow for appropriate works to take place. State management of potential lands that may need to be compulsorily purchased in the interest of facilitating provision of infrastructure could significantly reduce land acquisition costs. This reduced cost could speed up the process and make projects viable where they may have previously been deemed unfeasible.

Previous initiatives by NAMA to stimulate the housing market through intervention by way of a 'mortgage enhancement scheme' is an encouraging sign that the agency may be open to negotiating the inclusion of new niche activities, beyond its current remit, in the future. The expansion of NAMA's role beyond that of monetary return and in the interest of social gain could present a creative window of opportunity for the Irish State. NAMA could be the catalyst to facilitating meaningful collaboration across governmental departments to strategically tackle an array of interrelated local economic development factors.

Conclusion

Although it is still relatively early in the lifetime of NAMA to draw conclusions as to its level of impact on local economic development, it is unquestionably the case that NAMA activities do affect the potential of local economic development. Any assessment of the extent of that effect have to take account of a number of variables, including the potential to amend existing legislation, the rate of economic recovery, the uptake of development overstock, and demographics.

The health of our economy relies to an important degree on LED potential and the capacity to enhance local economic development potential, thereby encouraging economies of scale to support bigger and better investment. NAMA was designed to achieve gains on a national level, its interest in 'local' and 'district' is not particularly strong. The potential for local economic development is of course also related to how NAMA performs overall - the achievements of the agency come 2020. However, this assessment of performance is also proving to be a difficult one to define given the easily distorted values and gains of NAMA accounting mechanisms (namawinelake, 2012).

With regard to the potential for local economic development in the coming years, there is no doubt that the principle obstruction to local economic development has been the level of unsustainable localised planning practices across the State combined with the impact of the economic downturn. Negative impacts on local economic development which come as a direct result of NAMA activities are most likely to be seen in urban centres on city fringes where assets critical to economic prospects are now in NAMA management.

The fact that NAMA is not a national debt collector nor a national 'bad bank' but an asset management agency acting on behalf of the Irish public, provides scope for the development of a more enterprising, long term and accountable approach to the management of public assets. Since it has become apparent that the NAMA banks are experiencing a credit problem far more complex than initially thought, NAMA's core mission now lies in simply not making a loss on their purchased loans. Methods of employing state resources have had to become increasingly innovative, supporting a new consciousness of the economic importance of local capital. Surely then, a logical opportunity is presented to adjust NAMA legislation to enhance the potential gains for local economic development?

CHAPTER 8
ENTERPRISE ZONES: THE ENGLISH EXPERIENCE AND LESSONS FOR IRELAND

Andrew Moore

Introduction
When coming to power in May 2010, the Conservative-Liberal Democrat Government in the UK set about introducing a number of changes to the way spatial planning operates in England. Soon after entering government they abolished regional planning, leaving spatial planning to focus solely at sub-regional and local levels. At the same time, the government set out plans to give local communities new powers to steer the future planning and development of their areas. These changes emerged from Conservative Party pre-election proposals (Conservative Party, 2010a) and were promoted under the banners of Localism and Big Society. Localism was defined as devolving more power to local government, while giving communities a greater say in its form and function, enabling these communities to determine spending priorities and share in local growth (Conservative Party, 2009). This idea of Localism was later encapsulated within a broader aim, known as Big Society, which also included ideas such as empowering greater self-reliance and self-sufficiency among local communities, against a background of proposed public sector reform and support for social enterprise (Conservative Party, 2010b).

In many respects, these recent shifts in policy focus to the local level in England, mirror the last time that the British Conservative Party came to power at a time of economic crisis in the late 1970s. Then, as now, the Conservatives shifted government policy away from a strategic regional planning focus that prioritised depressed peripheral regions, towards a more targeted sub-regional and local intervention focus on depressed urban areas, in all parts of England. Although these policy changes were not then, as now, accompanied by any aim to empower local communities and social enterprise, they did share the same desire more generally to reduce the size of government and the public sector, while deregulating markets to encourage the private sector, among other things, to create jobs and meet public service needs.

This aim to facilitate private sector growth in the late 1970s, as with today, is evidenced by the rolling out of policies that focus on local spatial interventions to facilitate job creation in areas of urban deprivation. Of particular note in this regard is the use of spatially designated Enterprise Zones, which offer favourable planning and financial conditions, over a set number of years, to businesses that are established in or move to these areas.

This chapter begins by examining the use of Enterprise Zones in England over the course of the 1980s and 1990s. This allows for an understanding of how the policy was implemented and how it performed. The following sections provide a brief consideration of the new Enterprise Zone policy currently being implemented in England, and a discussion of what lessons can be learnt with regard to the effectiveness of Enterprise Zones as a locally focused spatial planning intervention tool.

Introduction to Enterprise Zones

From the early 1980s the British Government established Urban Development Corporations (UDCs), with the power to develop and regenerate deprived sub-regional areas, outside the normal planning system. Initially these were established only in Merseyside and the London Docklands, but subsequently eleven additional areas were designated between 1987 and 1993, ranging from Tyne and Wear in the north-east to Plymouth in the south-west. UDC operations were financially facilitated through Urban Development Grants from central government, with the explicit purpose of levering in private investment. Accompanying this sub-regional approach of targeted economic interventions, the Conservatives also introduced a more locally focused spatial planning policy known as Enterprise Zones (EZs).

The purpose of EZs was to secure the economic and physical regeneration of problem areas that were resistant to solutions by market forces or traditional planning policy instruments. Each EZ would therefore target measures to tackle different aspects of economic stagnation concurrently, in order to create synergies, positive externalities and ultimately a critical mass that could sustain long term interest from businesses and developers. In theory, this would be accompanied by the creation of jobs for local unemployed people through inward investment and new company start-ups (Potter and Moore, 2000).

Table 8.1: Enterprise Zone Round, by Number of Enterprise Zones Established

Enterprise Zone Round		Number of Enterprise Zones Established
One	1981-82	11
Two	1983-84	14
Three	1989-96	7

Thirty-two EZs were set up in three rounds (see Table 8.1). Each EZ ran for ten years, although four did receive extensions of two to four years. EZs were managed by a zone authority (either the local government authority or UDC) (Cullingworth and Nadin, 2006), which often targeted public investment to infrastructure upgrades and site promotion. In spatial terms, EZs were relatively small, up to 450 hectares in size, usually consisting of vacant, unoccupied or deteriorating industrial land, which was typically spread over several sites (Potter and Moore, 2000).

A number of financial and bureaucracy reduction incentives were offered in order to encourage businesses to establish in, or move to a designated EZ. These included exemption from; local business rates, Development Land Tax, Industrial Training Board levies and duties on re-exported goods for the lifetime of the EZ; and extra capital allowances against tax liabilities arising from property investment in the EZ. The incentives afforded by a reduction in bureaucracy were a simplified planning regime, outlining permitted development and providing speedier decisions; the fast tracking of applications for customs facilities; and a reduction in other bureaucracy and paperwork requirements.

A Framework for Examining Enterprise Zones
As the EZ policy was being introduced, several authors questioned the ability of EZs to succeed (see for example Butler, 1981; Clarke, 1982; Massey, 1982). Drawing on these authors, it is possible to discern a number of headline concerns that were raised by academics at that time. These included:

Investment and Job Creation
That EZ would be unable to attract investment and create jobs.

Appropriateness of Incentives
That the incentives on offer were inappropriate and did not address important issues regarding location (such as labour supply and public transport), while favouring investment in capital as opposed to labour.

Quality of Jobs and Distribution
Due to the incentives on offer, the quality of jobs created by inward investment would likely be poor in terms of skill level and remuneration, while there would be no guarantee that unemployed people living in the vicinity of EZs would gain a significant proportion of any new jobs created.

Business and Job Displacement
EZs would most likely become predominantly occupied by local and regional businesses, relocating jobs over short distances, which in turn could displace established local firms and jobs.

Local Embeddedness
In addition there would be no guarantee that new businesses would become locally embedded; for example through the development of strong links with local suppliers.

(Adapted from Potter and Moore, 2000)

Each of these areas of concern provides a useful lens through which to consider the performance of EZs. Since these questions were posed, there has been a dearth of comprehensive assessments regarding the effectiveness of EZs in England. While there have been many studies on the impact, outcome etc. of individual EZs (see for example Tyler's study on the Isle of Dogs EZ, 1993; Talbot's study of Tyneside EZ, 1988), very few studies have attempted to offer a comparative assessment of the overall nature and performance of EZs and directly address the above concerns.

Only two comprehensive studies have been carried out to assess the impact of EZs in England. The first was a longitudinal study commissioned by the British Government to examine EZ performance in bringing about physical regeneration and creating extra economic activity (PA Economic Consultants, 1987, 1995), which provided a generally positive view. The second study, carried out by Potter and Moore (2000; Moore and Potter 2002), focusing on the role of inward investors, provided a more nuanced overview of the strengths and weaknesses of EZs. Drawing on these studies, among others, this chapter will now turn to assessing the performance of EZs through the five headline concerns listed above.

The Performance of Enterprise Zones

Investment and Job Creation

Contrary to concerns regarding the ability of EZs to create jobs, it was estimated in the mid-1990s that the policy had resulted in 58,000 additional jobs, at a cost to the public sector of about £17,000 per job (£27,500 as of 2012). EZ firms were predominantly small in employee numbers, two-thirds having less than 20 employees and 85% having less than 50. Only 8% of firms employed more than 100 people. Most EZ firms were involved in manufacturing (45%), followed by distribution (17%) and retail (16%) (PA Economic Consultants, 1995).

Table 8.2: Enterprise Zone Business Type by % of Firms and % of Jobs

Business Type	% Firms	% Jobs
Relocation or Establishment of Branch/Subsidiary	66	72
New Company Starts	23	9
Pre-Designation Firms	11	19

(Source: Potter and Moore, 2000:1287 - adapted)

As illustrated in Table 8.2, EZs consisted predominantly of businesses that were either relocations or new establishments of branches/subsidiaries that were headquartered elsewhere. Such firms accounted for the majority of jobs created, by a large margin. Just under a quarter of EZ firms were indigenous to the EZ in terms of being 'New Company Starts'. This category also tended to be smaller in terms of job creation, accounting for just 9% of jobs. Considering these two categories together in relation to pre-designation firms (i.e. firms existing in the EZ prior to designation), can give an idea of the additional value that EZ designation brought to an area, indicating a ten-fold increase in the number of businesses and a five-fold increase in the number of jobs.

This picture of EZ effectiveness, however, was not evenly distributed, as different EZs developed with different strengths and weaknesses, influenced not only by the investment promotion focus of the zone authority, but also by the geographical context in which zones were established. Therefore, the nature and type of businesses found in EZs was also dependent on whether the EZ was located in an urban core area, in an accessible area outside an urban centre or in a remote rural area (Potter and Moore, 2000). For example, EZs in accessible areas were the most successful at attracting business relocations and branch/subsidiary establishments, which accounted for 73% of their firms and 78% of their jobs at time of de-designation (i.e. when EZ status was ended). This was followed by EZs in urban core areas (65% of firms and 57% of jobs) and remote rural areas (50% of firms and 70% of jobs). Newly established businesses were also found in greater numbers in accessible and urban core EZs, although they accounted for a greater proportion of businesses in rural EZs (33%) (Ibid.).

The spatial context of EZs also influenced the rate at which jobs were created and the type of economic sector that predominated. While accessible EZs showed steady growth throughout their existence, urban core zones did not show an appreciable increase in job creation until their fifth year. This has been attributed to the greater public infrastructure (and sometimes decontamination) work required to make such sites suitable for investment. Urban core EZs also tended to attract greater levels of retail and distribution job investment, due to the comparative advantage of the location of such sites, whereas manufacturing investment was more likely to be focused in accessible and remote zones, where larger and more flexible sites were available. Spatial context showed little impact on the location of service sector investment, which was evenly distributed across all zone types (Ibid.).

While spatial context helps to illuminate some of the differences in investment and job creation across EZs, it does not tell us much about why so many firms chose to invest and locate in EZs and why manufacturing predominated. To understand this, it is necessary to consider the scope and focus of EZ incentives.

Appropriateness of Incentives
The incentives offered to locate in EZs were favoured to varying degrees by investors (see Table 8.3). By far the most popular

inducement was relief from local business rates for the lifetime of the zone. Capital allowance tax benefits were favoured by just over one fifth of investors, followed by the relaxation of planning controls at 9%. The latter two incentives tended to be more popular among larger, manufacturing orientated investors who, according to Potter and Moore (2000), were more likely to build their own premises. Taking this into account, one can see that for the majority of smaller EZ investors, the single primary reason to locate in an EZ was local rates relief; the remaining EZ inducements provided little additional incentive.

Table 8.3: EZ Incentives Influencing Firms to Invest

EZ Incentive	% Firms
Rates relief	61.6
Capital allowance tax benefits	21.7
Relaxation of normal planning controls	8.9
Reduced statistical requirements	4.5
Other zone measures	4.6

(Source: Potter and Moore, 2000:1296 – adapted)

There were, however, other factors intrinsic to EZs, in terms of their spatial context and physical make-up (i.e. attributes) that influenced investors to locate there (see Table 8.4). Although none of these attributes were as popular as the rates relief incentive, premises availability was more favoured than capital allowance tax benefits.

Table 8.4: EZ Attributes Influencing Investors

EZ Incentive	% Firms
Non-EZ government incentives	9.0
Premises availability	26.8
Land availability	15.0
Supply to other businesses in EZ	5.8
Purchase from other businesses in EZ	0.9
Co-operate with other businesses in EZ	2.9
Attractive physical environment	17.7
Available labour force	15.8

(Source: Potter and Moore, 2000:1296 – adapted)

The availability of a local labour force was a factor for just under 16% of firms locating in EZs, with an attractive physical environment being marginally more popular at just under 18%. Taking these figures along with land availability (15%) and other non-EZ government incentives such as Regional Selective Assistance (9%), Potter and Moore (2000) attribute these scores to larger, manufacturing orientated investors, particularly in accessible and rural EZs. Sissons and Brown (2011) raise concerns in this regard, pointing to EZ attributes as essentially favouring investors who needed physical assets to operate, as opposed to facilitating the growing knowledge economy through the provision of incentives such as tax allowances for investment in research and development.

If one excludes the small group of larger manufacturing investors from the above figures, it is clear that the majority of EZ investors were primarily motivated by relief from local business rates, suggesting that other tax breaks in terms of rent, skilled labour and market access, may be more appropriate EZ incentives for smaller investors (Sissons and Brown, 2011). This raises questions regarding the suitability of EZ incentives and attributes, in that they were generally targeted at firms of any size and were, therefore, not sufficiently nuanced to meet the more pressing financial needs of smaller firms.

Job Quality and Distribution

EZs appear to have performed well in terms of job quality and local employment recruitment. For example, on average, about 20% of the workforce of EZ businesses consisted of management, professionals and technologists, with an additional 18% consisting of skilled manual and technical positions. With regard to local recruitment, Potter and Moore (2000) reported that the majority of EZ firms recruited most of their work forces locally, across a range of employment categories. As illustrated in Table 8.5, EZ firms scored very highly when it came to recruiting the majority of their administrative, skilled, semi-skilled and unskilled workers locally. In contrast, however, just over half of firms were recruiting more highly skilled professionals locally.

Table 8.5: Percentage of EZ Firms Recruiting the Majority of Different Parts of their Workforce Locally

EZ Firms' Employees Mostly Recruited Locally	% Firms
Managers	57
Professionals and Technologists	51
Administrative and Clerical Staff	89
Skilled Manual and Technical Workers	84
Semi-skilled Manual Workers	94
Unskilled Workers	95

(Source: Potter and Moore, 2000:1297 – adapted)

Larger investors from beyond the local area were the worst performers in terms of local recruitment of higher skilled professionals. These were typically branches or subsidiaries of firms headquartered elsewhere. The reason for their poor performance in this regard may be because such firms tend to concentrate management and technical tasks in head office (Watts, 1987), particularly in retail and manufacturing (Moore and Potter, 2002), which also explains why these larger investors also tended to have a higher proportion of lower-skilled employees.

While the overall lower proportion of higher skilled professionals recruited locally requires consideration, it is also important to note that EZs were specifically established in local areas of deprivation. Viewed from this perspective, Potter and Moore (2000) suggest that a larger number of lower skilled positions were required if EZs were to create jobs that matched the skills profile of the local population, which typically would not have had large numbers of higher skilled professionals. It is also important to note in this context that 35% of the recruits in EZ firms had been previously unemployed, which suggests positive local impacts of increased access to the job market.

Business and Job Displacement
As illustrated in Table 8.2, 66% of the firms located in EZs involved an establishment of a branch/subsidiary or a relocation of a firm already in existence elsewhere. Such firms accounted for 72% of the jobs created in EZs. More than three quarters of these firms had transferred to their EZ either from within the local area or region (Potter and Moore, 2000).

These statistics question the apparent success of EZs in the context of job and business creation in deprived areas. This is not surprising, when one considers reported displacement figures such as 25% of jobs within the same town (Ibid.) and 86% of firm relocations within the same county (Sissons and Brown, 2011). A study by Papke (1993) during the second round of EZs estimated that only about 25% of the jobs created in EZs were new jobs, suggesting a large displacement of business activity over short distances. Such displacement was most common among smaller firms, which tended to be concentrated in services, distribution and retail and was strongest in urban core EZs. Knock on displacement of the firms that already existed in the vicinity of EZs was also likely, evidenced by the fact that firms who moved to EZs were moving into local areas where on average 36% of their competitors were located (Potter and Moore, 2000).

Although EZs were designed to favour one area over another in order to target and stimulate a specific local economy, these very inducements appear to have encouraged a large number of businesses to relocate from elsewhere within the same locality or region. This raises questions about the apparent success of any EZ and the real and much larger cost to the public purse in terms of per job creation. It also suggests, according to Sissons and Brown (2011), the potential risk of EZs to destabilise established local economies as businesses are encouraged to locate in areas that have already been deemed less competitive in both spatial and economic contexts. In this way EZs can distort local markets, potentially leading to greater economic and social costs (Sissons and Brown, 2011).

Local Embeddedness of EZ Businesses

Apart from the value that EZ firms can bring to an area through jobs and new businesses, they can also bring considerable value depending on how embedded they become commercially within the local area. This can be measured through the level of EZ firm sales to customers outside the local area, which brings income into the local area, and the degree to which such firms purchase locally, therefore keeping income within the locality.

Table 8.6: EZ Firms' Customer and Supplier Linkages

Customer / Supplier Linkages	%
Amount of sales to customers abroad	7

Amount of sales to customers outside the local area	67
Level of purchases, by value, from local suppliers	23

(Source: Potter and Moore, 2000:1299 – adapted)

As illustrated in Table 8.6, 74% of sales to customers by EZ firms came from outside the local area, suggesting that the presence of EZ firms has been beneficial to their respective local areas. In contrast, however, EZ firms made just 23% of their purchases from local suppliers, suggesting rather weak performance in retaining income benefits locally (Potter and Moore, 2000). This high export / low local purchase pattern could be explained in part by the dominance of the subsidiary / relocation nature of EZ firms (67%), in which there may be more awareness of non-local supply and sales opportunities (Watts, 1987); and also by the high level of manufacturing (45%) among EZ firms, which can have specialised inputs and outputs that are less likely to be available from or destined for the local area (Potter and Moore, 2000).

Taking these findings together, with the evidence from Table 8.4 that very few firms investing in EZs were influenced by opportunities to supply to (just under 6%), co-operate with (just under 3%) or purchase from other local firms (just under 1%), would appear to suggest a relatively low level of local embeddedness among EZ firms. It has been suggested that embeddedness can take time to develop and that there were positive signs in this direction, evidenced by the fact that although 24% of firms said they intended to leave the EZ after financial benefits were ended, over two thirds of such firms intended to remain within the local area (Potter and Moore, 2000).

Enterprise Zones Revisited
The EZ policy was discontinued after New Labour came to power in 1997. Under their tenure the Office of the Deputy Prime Minister (ODPM) commissioned a study to assess transferrable lessons from the EZ policy (ODPM, 2003). The subsequent report broadly endorsed EZs as a tool for local economic intervention and addressed only some of the concerns raised above. It suggested continuing many aspects of the EZ policy as previously implemented, including capital grant tax allowances; investment in infrastructure; a relaxed planning regime; and the inclusion of spare land capacity to enable growth. The report did, however, propose a number of amendments to the policy, in order to address concerns regarding local economic distortion and the local labour context. It suggested that future EZs should not be solely

determined on the basis of deprivation, but rather on broader considerations of potential economic sustainability. New EZs could therefore assist with job creation in deprived areas through providing transport links to these areas, while also ensuring that proper skills and training were available to such communities. The report also recommended that any future EZs should consist of a range of site types and tenures, across a broader area, in order to minimise the potential for market distortions.

Subsequent to this report, the Conservative–Liberal Democrat coalition government of 2010 reintroduced EZs in England, designating twenty five new EZs during 2011 and 2012. Local areas were encouraged, through their Local Enterprise Partnerships (LEPs)[39], to bid for EZ designations through the incentive of being able to retain all business rates receipts that will accrue for up to twenty five years, with potential allowances for tax increment financing against these (Communities and Local Government, 2011). More generally, the policy approach to these new EZs took on board all of the suggested transferable lessons from the 2003 ODPM study. In particular, the policy emphasised that new EZs should be designated on the basis of genuine economic opportunity as opposed to deprivation, matching EZs with the economic priorities of the wider area. The new EZ policy was also introduced with a number of additional changes, requiring a LEP with a designated EZ to develop a plan, illustrating clearly additional economic growth and employment, while also being sensitive to displacement through the targeting of business growth that is genuinely additional (Communities and Local Government, 2011).

Discussion

While it is encouraging that the new approach to EZs in England has attempted to address many of the concerns raised earlier in this chapter regarding the impact of the policy during the 1980s and 1990s, it is not yet clear how effective the new policy changes will be. While it may be reassuring to think that the existence of an EZ plan will ensure that displacement is minimised, and only genuine additional economic and employment growth facilitated, there is no guarantee that this will be

---

[39] There are 39 Local Enterprise Partnerships across England. They are local business led partnerships between local authorities and businesses. They play a central role in determining local economic priorities and undertaking activities to drive economic growth and the creation of local jobs (lepnetwork.net).

the case and in fact, it is not yet clear how LEPs will go about delivering this. For the new approach to EZs to be effective and to avoid the mistakes of the past, would require a policy focus by LEPs specifically on new business start-ups, businesses that are genuinely expanding and larger inward investors; specifications which appear to be lacking.

In light of the evidence presented above, it could be reasonably assumed that the majority of businesses availing of the new EZ policy in England will most likely be doing so on the basis of business rates relief and capital tax allowances. This underlines a missed opportunity for other types of tax allowances that could favour research and development more generally, or those that could favour smaller, growing firms with regard to rent, skilled labour and market access. It also seems apparent, in light of previous experience, that there is little the renewed British EZ policy can do in terms of creating greater local embeddedness of EZ firms, particularly in relation to supply chains and business cooperation.

An even greater concern in relation to the EZ policy as it currently stands is that there appears to have been little critical engagement within government circles of the policy. The policy has been reintroduced with a public narrative that it has been improved. This is not to imply that the intentions of the policy are misplaced or that some of its economic intervention tools cannot produce some positive results, but rather to question the way the policy has been constructed and re-constructed. In essence, the English approach to EZs continues to operate as a broad and general set of measures to encourage local economic development. The same approach is applied to very different areas, each with their own unique socio-economic circumstances and is targeted at all business types and sizes, across all economic sectors. In addition, the development of EZs is no longer solely focused on areas of deprivation, but can now be any area with economic potential. In some respects, the new approach to EZs in England could be described as the favouring of twenty-five local area economic development plans by central government on the basis of their economic potential, through the awarding of favourable tax allowances and bureaucracy exemptions for a time limited period. The original central concern of addressing deprivation has been side-lined, making the EZs a general patch work, catch-all policy for local economic development, which, according to Marlow, gives little clarity as to how the benefits of an EZ will be spread across its wider LEP area (Marlow, 2011). Marlow has also raised valid concerns regarding the transparency of how the current round of EZs were chosen by central government, as well as questions surrounding the choice of EZ sites at local level, which has inevitably favoured particular land owners and developers over others (Marlow, 2011).

Despite the move of English EZ policy from the exclusive deprivation focus of the 1980s and 1990s to the current focus on areas of opportunity, it continues to take a scatter gun approach to local economic development, supporting and favouring all economic possibilities in a set number of land sites, within a time limited period, to the exclusion of all other locations in the country. In many respects, this contradicts the entire Localism ethos of the current British administration, as any desire to truly empower local communities would ensure that national policy on local economic development provides incentives that are available to all local areas and communities to use to their perceived advantage. The British government may be more effective in assisting and supporting local economic development in England if it provided a range of incentives, across a broader set of public policies, including educational, entrepreneurial, business and infrastructure development, in addition to a range of taxation incentives to encourage new and expanding businesses in general. Their current lack of regional and national planning perspectives might also benefit from some level of coordination of national economic development, in the context of Ireland, where Forfás have suggested that a multi-polar approach with different regional specialisations may be a more appropriate route for national economic development. Indeed, in addressing the British context, Sissons and Brown (2011) have suggested that specialised cluster development has been the only effective targeting of an EZ style local economic interventionist approach.

This discussion inevitably leads to a consideration of the ability of any local level of government in England or indeed Ireland, to deliver local economic development when there is such a range of disaggregated policy and institutional approaches[40]. Ó Riordáin

---

[40] See also: http://www.ahrrga.gov.ie/rural/rural-development/rural-economic-developm ent-zone-redz. A key outcome of the Commission for Economic Development of Rural Areas (CEDRA) is the *Rural Economic Development Zones (REDZ)*. These are functional rather than administrative geographic areas that reflect the spatial patterns of local economic activity.

(Chapter 9) addresses these concerns, suggesting that the local institutional capacity of an area should be strongly considered in the development of any local economy, alongside a range of other factors including local leadership and social inclusion. These are factors which appear to not have been considered by the current British government in its approach to local economic development through EZs.

CHAPTER 9
PLACING LOCAL GOVERNMENT AT THE HEART OF ECONOMIC RENEWAL

Seán Ó Riordáin

Introduction

The local government system in Ireland is one of the smallest in the OECD. There is a common perception of a country overloaded with local councillors and authorities. The reality, however, is that Ireland has relatively fewer councillors than all other EU countries, while its spending is near the bottom of the table[41]. There were 34 county and city councils with another 80 borough and town councils, making a total of 114 authorities in the Republic of Ireland prior to the Local Government Reform of 2014. The average population size per council was 39,190 albeit that this included the town and borough councils. The average size at County/City level, a more relevant comparator, given the range of functions of other European local government systems, was 131,412 people. This figure was only exceeded by the United Kingdom. Average spending in 2010 was €2,791 per person or 16% of public expenditure. Only Austria, Greece, Malta, Luxembourg and Cyprus had a smaller proportion of spending.

The Local Government Efficiency Review Implementation Group Report (2010) noted that day-to-day spending by city and county authorities in that year ranged from €783 per person to €1,889 per person. Spending by town and borough councils ranged from €927 per person to €7 per person! Furthermore, the level of discretion over that spending is limited by pre-determined and nationally driven obligations such as the provision of water and waste water facilities, national roads and other national infrastructure. The focus on such infrastructure has traditionally limited the scope for local flexibility on local spending priorities including, for example, economic development.

Nonetheless, and despite the widely held, if slightly inaccurate, belief that the range of functions of the Irish local government system is limited by comparison with other local government systems, it is clear

---

[41] EU sub-national governments 2009 key figures: Dexia/CCRE, February 2011 Brussels.

that Irish local authorities do play a critical role in the local economic arena. Currently, local government in Ireland has a mandate to:

- Provide a local democratic framework and through it an entry to national politics;
- Provide the local representational role and underpin local identity;
- Provide direct public services to residents, visitors and investors within a local context;
- Deliver, on an agency basis for the state, national services more appropriately delivered at a local level;
- Facilitate public and private investment;
- Provide the spatial planning context within which future development takes place;
- Provide the local platform through which social and cultural diversity is facilitated and nurtured;
- Regulate, in various instances, economic and environmental issues as well as providing local consumer protection;
- Facilitate, on behalf of the state, the co-ordination of local, rural and community development.

(Ó Riordáin, 2007)

Implementation of the above responsibilities is essential to the work of local and national development agencies. More particularly such functions are a cornerstone of a sustainable community, a central feature of which is a community which is economically viable. Local government thus has a mandate to support economic development.

This mandate is further strengthened through the provisions of the Local Government Reform Act (2014) which provides councillors with stronger policy making powers and a greater level of control over the actions of the local authority chief executive. The Act also places a greater emphasis within local authorities on the economic development of their communities through the establishment of the Local Community Development Committees, the drafting of the Local Economic and Community Plans and the inclusion of the Local Enterprise Offices within the remit of the authorities.

The key structural changes can be summarised as follows;

- The number of local authorities has been reduced from 114 to 31;

- The number of elected members has reduced from 1,627 to 949;
- The 80 town councils have been dissolved;
- 95 municipal districts have been established;
- 8 regional authorities and 2 regional assemblies have been replaced by 3 regional assemblies; and,
- The number of regional members has been reduced from 290 to 83.

As acknowledged earlier, traditionally local authorities have focused on infrastructural support across a range of areas – transport, environment, housing and roads. More recently social infrastructure, recreational/tourism infrastructure, and in many locations, broadband and urban and village renewal and related improvements have featured in their strategic economic role. Local government support for economic development also extends to a general mandate, established under the Local Government Act 2001, to improve the quality of life in local areas. These related areas of infrastructure provision and quality of life enhancement remain key foundations for economic development, and they continue to play a critical role in making local areas as attractive as possible to businesses and highly-skilled and sought after employees. This mandate to support local economic development was further extended through the Local Government Reform Act (2014).

Irish local authorities differ significantly in their geographical sizes and population levels and in the development issues they have to address. There is limited scope for comparing the role of the Dublin authorities with those generally around the country, even including County Cork. The need for development in the Greater Dublin Area has to be seen in the context of Greater Dublin being an international region in its own right competing with other international city-regions. The rest of the country can be placed within a development environment which can be characterised as national, with sub-national priorities; competing for international economic development while also facilitating indigenous enterprise. Thus, local authorities in the rest of the country play a supporting role, rather than being at the forefront of addressing the competitiveness of the Dublin Region in an international environment.

Irish local authorities, unlike their counterparts in other jurisdictions, have not traditionally had a direct responsibility for the areas of enterprise development, training, mentoring, and grant support, something that is a normal feature of the work of local authorities in other OECD countries. Indeed in some, such as Germany, the active engagement by local authorities in the provision of services, based upon commercial market pricing, facilitates local service provision and the reduction of local taxes. Despite not having a direct responsibility prior to the Local Government Reform Act (2014), there are nonetheless, many examples in Ireland of local authorities taking it upon themselves to engage in economic development. Recent initiatives illustrating how the economic development role has evolved across the local government sector include:

- Business Support Units / Economic Development Units set up in each county / city council to act as points of contact for businesses to ensure local authority services and activities contribute to economic development and job creation;
- Development and operation of business parks / enterprise centres, addressing infrastructure deficits where these cause particular problems to businesses;
- Establishment of tourism initiatives / companies to develop and market local tourism products;
- Support for small, medium and large-scale cultural events and festivals designed to attract people to the area, with significant spin-offs for local businesses;
- Support for practical initiatives to respond to business closures which having had a local impact – for example liaising with employees to assess needs and opportunities, identifying skill sets, providing information supports to those seeking employment elsewhere or who wish to start their own business.

Some specific examples include:

- Development of a Tipperary Science and Technology Campus as a joint project of South Tipperary County Council, the IDA and Tipperary Institute;
- Development of the Western Greenway in Mayo underpinning a general development of looped walks across the County through partnership with the local development sector and the Department of Tourism;

- The Waterford City Tourism Initiative led by Waterford City Council with the support of Fáilte Ireland, Waterford Institute of Technology and local businesses which includes joint marketing, developing product offerings and The House of Waterford Crystal;
- Development of the Green Way - a green economic corridor initiated by an alliance of businesses, academic institutions and local authorities in the Dublin area which aims to position Ireland as a centre of cleantech innovation and enterprise which will link business to investors and develop trade partnerships with other major international green corridors;
- The development in Kilkenny of a research incubation facility as part of the Invest Kilkenny Initiative.

The local government system therefore has a positive track record in the sphere of local economic development. As these and other examples show, the foundation for local government to play a more active role in economic development was already laid prior to the Local Government Reform Act (2014).

Given the existing local government mandate to support the social, economic, environmental and physical development of local areas, and its work in supporting economic development to date, local government is seen by the OECD, the European Commission and best international practice generally, as the natural institutional setting for local economic development. This is recognised in the Programme for Government, 2011-2016 and in the Local Government Efficiency Review (2010) which noted that the business support role would be a natural complement to the wider economic development brief of local authorities.

If we are to learn from other countries which have undergone similar shifts in their economic models, perhaps the key role for local government in Ireland is in the use of the local government system to create the multi-agency environment in which micro-level enterprise can grow. It comes as no surprise that Ireland needs to develop an economic model based on a capacity to export goods and services where competiveness is as much about a capacity to innovate as it is about prices being set at market acceptable levels. In that context, when investors, foreign and indigenous, existing and potential, are considering investment in a particular manufacturing sector or service area, they take account of a number of critical features which will ultimately inform the decision to retain the investment, make a new investment or re-structure what may already be in place. These features are:

- Locational specific aspects related to social, political and environmental qualities;
- Institutional capacity of the area and the networks existing within the area;
- Delivery capacity of the area and its relationship to hierarchical economic frameworks, i.e. local, regional, national, international.

Given the above it is clear, from a strictly economic perspective, that companies, entrepreneurs and others can drive economic activity if the appropriate institutional framework is in place. It is now evident that much new development, as well as the continuation of existing economic activities, is dependent upon the adaptation of a community towards production and service delivery, and changes in processes that are increasingly influenced by the international market place. This requires active policy making rather than reactive or passive policy development which has been a feature of the more recent past.

Equally, however, it is increasingly evident that high performance enterprises of all scales are dependent upon locations having a high quality of life, the necessary social networks and supports, as well as a vibrant social and cultural outlook. Local authorities retain a responsibility in Ireland, and elsewhere, to ensure that this aspect of their mandate remains a central feature in their policy objectives to create an environment in which sustainable enterprise is a cornerstone of all communities throughout the state but very specifically in the Greater Dublin Region, given its role as the economic driver for the Country.

Key Competitiveness Issues that Need to be Addressed
In its review of the competitiveness of the Irish economy, The World Economic Forum has highlighted several areas that require attention at the local and national level if the economy is to reverse recent trends which mark a reduction in Ireland's overall level of competitiveness. It is not intended to analyse these in detail here and it is important to acknowledge that the international investor perception of Ireland did suffer, but increasingly Ireland is positioning itself to regain and build

upon a more positive environment. However, the need to address these competitiveness issues remain and local government does have a hand in ensuring that there is a co-ordinated approach to doing so at the local level:

Lack of Trust of Political Institutions
In general it is recognised that in recent years the public perception of government has been poor. Therefore, it is unsurprising that at the international level this is highlighted as one of the most significant inhibitors of Irish competitiveness. There is a challenge to the authorities, as national and local political institutions, to confront this perception and address it, regardless of the reasoning for these poor perceptions.

Local/National Regulatory Burdens
There is an on-going effort at national and local level to reduce regulatory burdens on industry and enterprise generally. Notwithstanding this, the challenge is to ensure that the regulatory environment complements international and local competitiveness, rather than inhibits the capacity to export or to trade internally in the state. A particular concern is acknowledged in regard to local planning and the need to ensure that it is adequately integrated with national and regional guidelines.

Poor Infrastructure
It is evident that considerable progress has been made in the development of the major inter-urban routes and in the Inter-City rail and bus services. However public transport in all the major Irish cities is seen as being in need of further investment to match the progress of other European cities. More specifically in Dublin, the need for more than adequate transport and telecommunications services, the availability of clean water, waste water and waste management are issues that are regularly highlighted by, among others, Forfás, the National Competitiveness Council, and more recently in the Programme for Government.

Access to Financing
The issue of creating alternative mechanisms to local financing and micro-financing has been flagged as an on-going challenge by the business sector, particularly for existing businesses. A positive

development in this regard is the operation of Local Enterprise Offices (LEOs) in each County.

Favouritism in Public Contracts

In some ways it is surprising to have this issue highlighted given the perception that the procurement system in Ireland is viewed within the public service as being very open. Nonetheless, it is an area where more action is required to ensure that there is an even playing pitch for both internal and external competitors for Irish contracts, including those at local level. Recent signals from the Department of Public Expenditure and Reform suggest that we are likely to see significant reform in the management of public procurement and that such reforms may well address this long-standing concern

Wasteful Public Spending

The need to ensure that the maximum value for public spend is achieved is, and will remain, a central feature of public expenditure at all levels of government for the foreseeable future. This is likely to include a look back requirement with regard to local capital programmes to ensure that the intended rate of return is achieved and accounted for.

Internet Access-Broadband

Broadband availability is an area which has been severely criticised in recent years. It is clear that, notwithstanding the progress of the past two years, much more remains to be addressed if Ireland is to live up to the challenge of the SMART economy. The NewERA proposals of Government identify this as a target investment area which is highlighted in the *Infrastructure and Capital Investment Plan 2016-2021.*

Local Availability of Research and Training Services

The transfer of local research efforts in the universities and other third level bodies to local economies is a distinct advantage in terms of adaptation to the prevailing international market conditions. Considerable investment is being made in civil research and development in Ireland, whilst other opportunities could arise, which free up entrepreneurs to move on ideas within companies or indeed through new start-ups. The capacity to translate for example, MBA project work, which is on-going across the state, into sustainable business ideas, could be an area worth considering.

Firm Level Technology Absorption

An on-going challenge is the need to develop indigenous investment to make greater use of new technology in an effort to move into an international market place. It is evident that where this has been attempted the business outcomes have been positive and can present greater opportunities to underpin local economic development.

A Local Role in Future Economic Development

Given the above, all those charged with economic development across the country will need to bear in mind the series of challenges that will confront business and economic development generally over the foreseeable future. Whilst it will be difficult against a backdrop of increasing constraints on local and national resources, the reality is that if the state development agencies and the local authorities fail to confront these challenges the economic environment will get worse and much of the solid progress of the past years will be lost.

This will be of particular importance to a local government system which is undergoing considerable re-structuring. In the move towards a national water utility, the migration of back-office services to a national arrangement, local authorities will be smaller, more streamlined and less focused on engineering-based services, with reduced budgets and discretion. Their remaining responsibilities will be focused on community and economic development services, local planning and housing.

The idea that local government would be responsible for local economic development is now well established within spatial economics and is generally found to be a central feature of innovation in and development of advanced economies throughout the OECD. In some instances, the institutional model is based upon a direct provider role for local government, in others the role is one of setting direction and providing leadership. In both, the role includes the application of sanction by the local authority, or failing that, by a national or regional body with responsibility for setting broad strategic direction, underpinned by clear output and outcome parameters for the local operators. The Local Government Reform Act (2014) enacted this change by abolishing the County Enterprise Boards and integrating the

Local Enterprise Offices, local development partnerships and other local initiatives into local government. A realignment of the local institutional setting is formally linked to the adoption of the Local Economic and Community Plan with an economic and community development unit in each local authority.

Such reforms of local arrangements in Ireland necessitates a significant change in the cultures of both local and national bodies. This is important, for one of the constant bugbears with regard to the reform of local government has been a history of mistrust of the system and its capacity to lead change. Such perspective has, in the past, provided a ready-made excuse for creating new local bodies and for isolating local government from the economic development role. If local government is to be successful following the reform process then it must be on the basis of it renewing its leadership role within the re-configured economic policy arena. This will be essential to sustaining a vibrant role as a community leader. It is also going to be vital to our economic future, particularly in Dublin, given its central role in the economic health of the nation. The worry is whether there is any awareness of the role local government plays in renewing lagging regions and whether we are in danger of sleep walking into even deeper trouble because of a concern to defend old ways of doing things and defending boundaries which have limited relevance to a 21st century economy.

CHAPTER 10
New Entrants and Inherited Competence – The Evolution of the Irish Biotech Sector

Declan Curran, Chris van Egeraat and Colm O'Gorman

Introduction

Explanations of the emergence and subsequent development of industries have become increasingly informed by evolutionary theory. This evolutionary perspective seeks to explain the clustering of industries in terms of the entry, growth, decline and exit of firms, and their locational behaviour (Boschma and Frenken, 2011). The economic evolution of firms facilitates the selective transmission and replication of firm-specific organisational routines, with spin-off firms and labour mobility being the primary vehicles for the transfer of increasingly modified routines (Nelson and Winter, 1982; Teece *et al.*, 1997). In this evolutionary characterisation of the industrialisation process, spin-off firms enable clusters of firms to be self-reproducing even in the absence of traditional Marshallian agglomeration economies, such as labour pooling, technological spill-overs, and local access to specialised suppliers (Klepper, 2007; Boschma and Wenting, 2007).

This line of research, focusing on the role of spin-off processes in industry evolution, has been strongly influenced by the work of Klepper (2008), who shows how organisational reproduction and inherited company traits can influence spin-off processes. Klepper's formal theoretical model of the evolution of industrial concentrations explains the process through which spin-off firms can lead to clustering in terms of these inherited company traits of organisational reproduction. He argues that firms differ innately in terms of their levels of competence, and the competence of firms is based on their pre-entry experience. In newly evolving industries new firms acquire their competence from firms in related industries and from prior entrants into the industry. In this way, clusters are characterised as emerging from a snowball process of spin-off formation. Spin-offs inherit a large part of their capabilities from their parent, which explains why successful firms tend to give birth to successful firms (Boschma and Frenken, 2011).

Do such explanations apply to knowledge-intensive sectors characterised by high numbers of new firms that are spin-offs from

Higher Education Institutes (HEIs)? One such industry is the modern biotechnology sector. A notable characteristic of the modern biotechnology sector is the presence of small dedicated biotech firms. In the aftermath of the US research programme, known as the human genome project (HGP), of the early 1990s, a biotechnology industry organisational structure emerged which featured small dedicated biotech firms at the heart of a complex innovation network. Specifically, the post-genome era is characterised by knowledge accumulation that is no longer being driven by large international corporations only. Rather, industry evolution and knowledge accumulation is now facilitated through a complex and interactive network of public research institutions, large international corporations, HEI start-ups and other research-orientated small biotech firms, and even consumer associations (Quéré, 2004).

More generally, the evolution of the global biotechnology industry over the last two decades has not been a uniform process across countries. Senker's 2004 study of how country-specific characteristics have impacted biotech industry development looked to Austria, France, Germany, Greece, Ireland, Netherlands, Spain and the UK. It found that differences in country-specific supply conditions and the existing national structure of production, such as the mix of domestic and foreign-owned firms; the level of biotech knowledge and skills; public policy for developing the science base; and cultural traditions in universities, can all lead to variations in the rate of small firm creation across national biotech sectors. What is more, cross-country differences in demand for, and social acceptance of, emerging biotechnological applications, can also impact upon the national pattern of biotech innovation. Of the eight European countries studied, the empirical analysis of Senker pointed to Germany, The Netherlands and the UK as having cultivated business environments rich in factors supportive of innovation (and free from factors which impede innovation) in the biotech industry. In the Irish case, while a long standing policy to support biotech innovation, technology transfer and small firm creation, as well as access to the EU market, were cited as positive factors, poor availability of finance capital and limited R&D skills were identified as negative factors (2004).

As discussed in Nosella et al. (2005) and Orsenigo (2001), among others, the biotechnology sectors of European countries (apart from the

UK) have developed at a much later stage than in the US[42]. These differences in the timing of evolution are typically explained in terms of differences in: (i) the availability of financing for new firms (such as in the absence of structured venture capital); (ii) the protection guaranteed by the patents system; (iii) the strength of HEI/industry relationship, and its implications for knowledge transfer; and (iv) the fragmentation and specialisation of research.

In this chapter, we explore the extent to which Klepper's theory can be usefully employed to understand the evolution of the Irish biotechnology sector, which is characterised by a large government funded investment in research in HEIs and by specific policies and supports aimed at commercialising such research through spin-offs. Our analysis shows that the industry has experienced two distinct evolutionary processes involving, on the one hand, HEI spin-offs, and on the other hand, private sector spin-offs.

The chapter is structured as follows: Section two provides a brief overview of the role of spin-offs in industry evolution. Section three details our research methods, data sources and definitions. Section four presents the evolution of the Irish biotech industry and the chronology of spin-offs. Section five compares the ability of spin-offs of private sector origins and HEI origins to attract venture capital funding. Finally, Section six concludes and sets out the policy implications of our findings.

The Role of Spin-Offs in Industry Evolution

Evolutionary perspectives have become increasingly prominent in explanations of industrial concentration and growth (Asheim, Cooke and Martin, 2006). The literature on regional and national innovation systems has been particularly influential (Cooke, 2001; Malerba, 2003; Lundvall, 1992; Edquist, 2005). These evolutionary approaches to understanding industry evolution and cluster development are characterised by a focus on innovation and learning processes, a historical perspective and an emphasis on the role of institutions and networks. As regards the explanation for the actual clustering process, moving away from a narrow focus on external economies of scale and pecuniary externalities, the evolutionary approaches tend to focus on the role of proximity in stimulating information flows and knowledge

---

[42] For a detailed treatment of the development of biotech firms in the Baltic countries and Poland, see Malo and Norus (2009).

spill-overs. However, recent evolutionary scholarship suggests that such factors may play only a limited role in driving industrial cluster processes, at least in the early stages, and call for a focus on spin-off processes (Boschma and Wenting, 2007; Ter Wal and Boschma, 2007).

A formal model of the evolution of industrial concentrations driven by spin-off processes has been developed by Stephen Klepper (2008 and 2010). The model has been applied to the US tyre industry in Buenstorf and Klepper (2009) and to Detroit's automobile industry and Silicon Valley's integrated circuits industry in Klepper (2010). The theory characterises industry evolution in terms of organisational reproduction and inherited company traits to explain how spin-off firms can lead to clustering. In this way, the theory emphasizes the internal spill-overs and hereditary characteristics inherent in individual firms, rather than external spill-overs accrued from close proximity to large concentrations of firms, as a driver of a given firm's long-term performance.

According to Klepper, firms differ innately in terms of their levels of competence, and the competence of firms is based on their pre-entry experience. He identifies three types of entrants into a new industry based on their pre-entry experience: firstly, diversifiers, which are entrants that diversify from related industries; secondly, spin-offs, which are founded by employees from incumbent firms; and thirdly, start-ups, which are founded by employees of firms in related industries or other capitalists with no experience in the new industry. Klepper postulates that the spin-offs will have the highest degree of competence, based on organisational and industry experience. Spin-offs can exploit knowledge about the new industry that their founders gained while working in the industry at their "parent" firms. They are expected to have inherited traits from these parents. Start-ups on the other hand are characterised by low competence, reflecting a lack of organisational and industry experience.

Thus a firm's pre-entry experience critically shapes its competence, and its performance then influences its competitiveness, its chance of survival and growth, and the rate at which it generates further spin-offs. Such spin-off processes are then an important factor in the explanation of industrial clustering processes because spin-offs tend to locate in relative proximity to their parent firm. In what follows, we use Klepper's theory to analyse the evolution of the Irish biotechnology sector.

Research Method, Data Sources and Definitions

We present a single case study of the evolution of the Irish biotech sector. The context for this study, the Irish biotech sector, is of interest for a number of reasons. First, a priori we know that the industry is characterised by many HEI spin-offs and by spin-offs from one firm, Elan Corporation, Ireland's most successful indigenous biotech firm. This initial entrant set up in a location with few (if any) existing entrants, went on to become an industry leader, and in time spun off firms. Second, over the period of this study there was a significant increase in public research funding for biotech research, and this was accompanied by specific policy measures aimed at commercialising that research. Third, the sector is important both internationally and in Ireland. The sector in Ireland comprises approximately 100 firms and accounts for employment of 3,000. Fourth, as noted above, the development of the biotech industry over the last two decades has not been a uniform process across countries (Nosella *et al.*, 2005; Orsenigo, 2001).

Partly due to the lack of official statistics and partly due to the ambiguous nature of the definition it is difficult to determine the size of the Irish biotech industry. Our 'universe' of firms in the modern biotech industry in Ireland is based on existing survey material, the list of firms included on the 'Biotechnology Ireland' website (hosted by Enterprise Ireland), information from interviews with industry experts and internet searches. Our data collection began with an inventorisation of biotech firms in Ireland. Following this, we compiled a dataset based on an extensive internet search of official company websites and media sources. The resulting dataset contains information on the founders of each firm; serial entrepreneurs who form numerous firms; and spin-off firms. The database also identifies whether these spin-off companies emerged from existing private firms or HEIs. The date of establishment of all spin-offs and existing firms is also included in the dataset, allowing us to undertake an analysis of the evolution of the Irish biotech industry over time. We verified the database through consultation with industry experts and with the information contained in the Bureau van Dijk *FAME* business database.

We have also collected data on the venture capital funding provided to Irish biotech firms over the period 2000-2010. We use data from the Irish Venture Capital Association (IVCA) (www.ivca.ie) for the period 2007-2010. IVCA data is available at firm-level across sectors, and the data source also identifies the investors who provided the funding to each firm contained in the dataset. We have extended this data back as far as 2000 for the biotech industry, based on the data we identified in The Irish Times Archive of business news.

Finally, it remains to clarify a number of definitional issues. We define modern biotechnology as per the OECD's (2006a) definition. The OECD employs a list based definition that includes various techniques and activities: synthesis, manipulation or sequencing of DNA, RNA or protein; cell and tissue culture and engineering; vaccines and immune stimulants; embryo manipulation; fermentation; using plants for clean-up of toxic wastes; gene therapy; bioinformatics, including the construction of databases; and nano-biotechnology.

Regarding the term "spin-off", it should be noted that multiple definitions exist for the terms spin-off and spin-out (for a discussion see Myint *et al.*, 2006) and the definitional issues are further confused by the fact that the meaning of the two terms tends to be inverted in Europe and the USA. Therefore, we only use the term spin-off and apply a broad definition that covers a wide range of firms, including: (1) firms started as the result of a mother-organisation splitting off existing units or departments and the mother company holding (at least initially) equity stakes in the new firm and (2) firms formed by employees or groups of employees leaving an existing organisation to form an independent start-up firm. The parent entity can be a firm, a HEI or another organisation. In the second case the firm is only considered a spin-off if the employees received some form of assistance/support/stimulation from the parent organisation or if they are based on intellectual property/core capability developed during the employees' stay at the parent organisation.

The Evolution of the Irish Biotech Sector

The Irish Biotechnology Sector
The development of the 'modern' biotech sector in Ireland took off in earnest in the 1990s, although substantial employment growth only occurred in the 2000s due to the establishment of a number of foreign-owned biopharmaceutical manufacturing plants. Applying the OECD (2006a) modern biotechnology definition, the inventorisation of the sector, undertaken for this study, has counted 99 indigenous biotechnology firms, of which 35 can be classified as HEI spin-offs, 33

as private sector spin-offs, and 31 as other private sector start-ups (Table 10.1). In terms of ownership most firms are Irish. Of the 35 HEI spin-offs, all started as Irish owned firms, though two have recently been acquired by foreign companies; of the 33 private sector spin-offs, seven are foreign-owned; while eight of the other private sector start-ups are foreign-owned. In terms of sector, biopharmaceuticals and bio-diagnostics are the largest subsectors, accounting for 64% of firms. Virtually all employment is concentrated in these sub-sectors (Van Egeraat and Curran, 2010). On the basis of firm-level data, available from the FAME database, and reports from industry experts we estimate that the Irish biotech industry employed just under 3,000 persons in 2009. The majority of indigenous firms are micro-enterprises, employing less than 10 staff. The majority of the university spin-offs are very small, early stage start-up or university campus based firms. Most of the indigenous bio-pharmaceutical companies are still at an embryonic stage, operating out of university labs, with less than one third of them having brought molecules beyond pre-clinical trials.

Table 10.1: Irish Biotech Sector Firm and Employment Distribution

	Biotech firm breakdown (%)	Biotech employment (%)	Average firm size (no. of employees)
University spin-offs	35%	10%	9
Private sector spin-offs (including those from Elan)	33%	46%	42
Other private sector start-ups	31%	44%	43

Source: FAME database and authors' calculations

Spin-off Processes in the Irish Biotechnology Sector
We now focus on the evolution of the Irish Biotech industry. Specifically, we distinguish between Irish biotech firms who originated as HEI spin-offs and Irish biotech firms of private sector origins, both private sector spin-offs and private sector start-ups, as per Klepper (2008). HEI spin-offs account for 35% of the firms in our dataset. The remaining firms originated in the private sector and are almost evenly

split between private sector spin-offs (33%) and other private sector start-ups (31%).

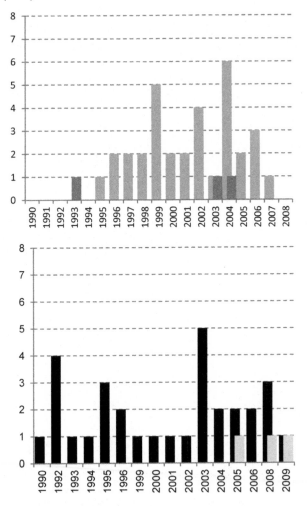

Source: FAME database

Figure 10.1: HEI Spin-Off Entrants and Exits (top) and Private Sector Spin-Off Entrant and Exits (bottom) 1990-2008

Notes: Entrants and exits above refer to the cohort of firms under observation in this study. Entrants are indicated by dark shading, while exits are indicated by light shading.

Figure 10.1 illustrates the chronology of HEI spin-off entrance and exit, as well as the entrance and exit of private sector spin-offs, over the period 1990-2008. It is apparent from Figure 10.1 that the incidence of biotech HEI spin-off begins circa 1995. Private sector spin-offs enter throughout the period 1990-2008, but occur with relatively more frequency in the early 2000s. The low incidence of exit observed in both HEI spin-offs and private sector spin-offs may be due to the fact that some biotech firms opt to remain dormant rather than exit the industry entirely in the hope that their research output may be acquired at a later stage.

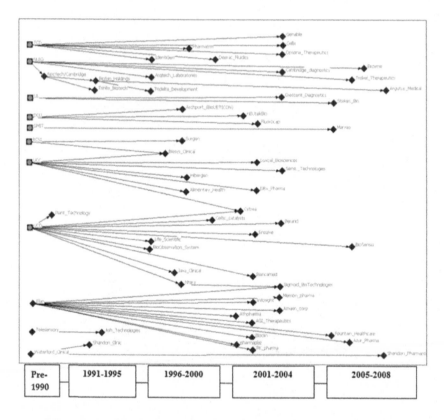

Figure 10.2: Chronology of Irish Biotechnology Spin-offs, 1990-2008

Note: HEIs denoted by circle-in-box; all companies denoted by diamond. This data suggests that the development of the Irish biotech industry is characterised by two distinct evolutionary processes involving, on the one hand, a series of private sector spin-offs that can be traced back to the founding of Elan, Ireland's largest indigenous biotech multinational, founded more than four decades ago, and, on the other hand, a more recent process of HEI spin-offs which has emerged over the last decade.

126

Focusing only on spin-offs, Figure 10.2 presents a more detailed genealogy of the Irish biotech sector, separating spin-offs in terms of their origins. HEI and private sector spin-off processes are largely separate processes, with only one spin-off identifiable as having both private sector and HEI origins. Subsequent waves of spin-offs have yet to emanate from those spin-offs created over the 1990-2008 period. HEI spin-offs occurred predominantly over the 1996-2004 period, and to a lesser extent over the 2005-2008 period. One firm, Elan, an indigenous Irish firm, is clearly the dominant source of private spin-offs, accounting for 12 spin-offs post-2001.

Evolutionary Path I: The Role of Elan

Elan Corporation was launched in 1969, when Elan founder, Donald Panoz, moved to Ireland from the United States. He had formerly been the founder of a successful drug delivery firm, Mylan laboratories, in Pittsburgh. It has been suggested that his choice to set up Elan in Ireland was influenced by the favourable tax regime and less restrictive bureaucracy in place in Ireland[43]. Originally a specialist in drug delivery systems, Elan initially provided drug absorption control technology for antibiotics produced by other global pharmaceutical companies. By the early 1980s, Elan had secured contracts for the provision of absorption technology for 25 pharmaceutical products from 16 different pharmaceutical companies. While continuing this contracting work, Elan also further developed its own research and development capabilities, and in 1992 the company became the first to receive Food and Drug Agency (FDA) approval for the transdermal nicotine patch.

In the 1990s Elan's interests extended into the area of neuroscience and the company subsequently undertook the development of its own products for the treatment of Alzheimer's disease, Parkinson's disease, and multiple sclerosis[44]. To facilitate this product development, Elan embarked on an aggressive acquisitions strategy. At the same time,

---

[43] See:http://www.fundinguniverse.com/company-histories/Elan-Corporation-PLC-Company-History.html.

[44] Elan's neuroscience drug discovery research is primarily carried out in the company's US-based laboratories. While Elan Corporation is headquartered in Dublin, Irish involvement has been largely confined to the development of drug delivery products in the Elan Drug Technologies unit in Athlone, Co. Westmeath. Elan also established a research group in Trinity College Dublin in 1990. In May 2011, US-based Alkermes agreed to purchase Elan Drug Technologies unit in a deal worth €960 million.

Elan began building a web of strategic partnerships, acquiring minority stakes in a number of companies that in turn paid the company licensing fees for its technology. However, Elan's stock market value collapsed in 2002 after the US Securities and Exchange Commission launched an investigation into the company's accounting practices. Elan responded by implementing a recovery plan which involved the divesting of a number of subsidiaries and licenses in an effort to drive down debt[45].

This divesture of biotechnology assets, accompanied by the departure of a substantial number of executives and scientists from Elan's Irish operations, has led to the emergence of a wave of Irish biotech firms that were either spun off from Elan or formed by former Elan staff. During the two-year period between 2002 and 2004 alone, nine firms were spun off and another three firms followed between 2005 and 2008. Other Elan alumni have dispersed into existing biotech and pharmaceutical firms, as well as into legal and venture capital firms (Sheridan, 2008).

The interconnectedness of former Elan staff is a prominent feature of these spin-offs. One of the first spin-offs in 2003, AGI Therapeutics, which adapts molecular entities for the treatment of gastrointestinal conditions, was founded by former Elan executive, John Devane. He had previously been a founder of Athpharma in 2001, which was acquired in 2006 by another former Elan executive, Seamus Mulligan. Seamus Mulligan then transferred its assets into a new venture called Circ Pharma, where he was joined by another former Elan executive, Peter Thornton. Seamus Mulligan also established specialty pharmaceutical firm Azur Pharma, which is managed by a number of former Elan executives (Daly, 2008). Peter Thornton is also a member of the board of Merrion Pharmaceutical. Established in 2004, this company acquired the oral drug delivery assets developed at Elan Biotechnology Research. In 2004 a management group led by Elan's former chief financial officer, Thomas Lynch, took over Amarin Corporation, following Lynch's purchase of Elan's stake in the firm (Sheridan, 2008).

---

[45] "The Story of Elan", *The Irish Times*, 29th October, 2010.

<u>Evolutionary Path II: The Role of Publically Funded Investment in HEIs</u>
In parallel with the wave of Elan spin-offs, since the mid-1990s Ireland
has witnessed a strong increase in HEI spin-offs. This development can
be linked to a substantial public sector investment over the last 10 years
which has contributed significantly to the biotech research performance
of Irish universities. This funding injection has been timely, given the
changing organisation of the global biotechnology industry in the post-
genome era and the enhanced opportunities for small scale HEI spin-
offs and dedicated biotech firms to explore new avenues of research,
into which larger integrated firms are unable or unwilling to allocate
resources. In 1998 the Irish government launched the Programme for
Research in the Third-Level Institutions (PRTLI) and Science
Foundation Ireland (SFI), which since its inception has invested €865
million (including exchequer and private matching funds) into
strengthening national research capabilities via investment in human
and physical infrastructure[46]. A biotech-related example of this public
sector funding is the SFI's recent investment of €10 million in the
Regenerative Medicine Institute (REMEDI) based in NUI Galway
(Ahlstrom, 2010).

A further effort aimed at cultivating HEI–industry linkages has been
the establishment of seven Centres for Science, Engineering and
Technology (CSET). One such CSET is the Biomedical Diagnostics
Institute (BDI), which brings together a partnership of five HEI
institutions and six companies[47]. The BDI was founded in 2005 through
SFI funding of €16.5 million and an additional €6.5 million provided by
industry partners. The process of technology transfer within Irish
universities has also evolved over the last decade. According to
Geoghegan and Pontikakis (2008), a significant empowerment of
Technology Transfer Offices of the Irish universities has occurred over
the last decade, in tandem with a rapid realignment of HEI research
activities. Figures 10.1 and 10.2 show how these policy initiatives paid
off. The number of HEI spin-offs has increased substantially since the
mid-1990s with a peak in 2004.

To summarise, Elan's divestiture of biotechnology assets and
product rights, as well as the dispersion of former Elan executives and
researchers throughout the Irish biotech industry, fundamentally
changed the trajectory of the industry. Prior to its restructuring

---

[46] See www.hea.ie for further details.
[47] For further information regarding the Biomedical Diagnostics Institute, see www.bdi.ie.

(necessitated by an accounting scandal), Elan was characterised by industry analysts as being "hermetically sealed from the rest of Ireland's indigenous life sciences industry" and as operating "on a different plane compared to the small-scale, undercapitalized ventures that otherwise constituted the sector" (Sheridan, 2008:39). A second, distinct process shaping the Irish biotechnology sector over the last decade has been the large-scale public sector investment aimed at developing the biotechnology research capabilities of HEIs and HEI spin-offs. The next section will analyse the relative success of the spin-offs arising from the two processes.

Venture Capital Funding in the Irish Biotechnology Sector
We now discuss the ability of the two spin-off groups to attract private sector funding. Klepper (2008) postulates that high competence parent firms give birth to high competence spin-off firms. Spin-offs can exploit knowledge about the new industry that their founders gained while working in the industry at their "parent" firms. They are expected to have inherited traits from these parents. We assess whether or not this "high competence parent, high competence spin-off" relationship can be detected in the flows of venture capital funding to spin-off firms within the Irish biotechnology sector.

The Irish biotech sector's development in recent years has been greatly shaped by the availability of private equity venture capital funding. Total venture capital investment in Ireland has more than doubled since 2002, while the Irish proportion of venture capital secured by the Irish biotech industry has also experienced a marked increase since 2002. Despite a more restrictive funding environment in 2009, venture capital funding for Irish biotech companies appears to have remained resilient over the 2002-2009 period. Of the total percentage of Irish venture capital, the biotech sector received slightly less than 2% in 2002, 13% in 2008, and 31% in 2009[48].

A breakdown of the venture capital invested in Irish biotech firms from 2000 to 2010 is provided in Figure 10.3. Private sector spin-offs were clearly the most successful in this regard, accounting for more than two thirds of all venture capital. Spin-off firms emanating from Elan have enjoyed notable success in attracting private sector

---

[48] Data calculated from PWC (2005), IVCA *Venture Capital Pulse*, 2007-2009 www.ivca.ie. All monetary figures are in current values. 2008 and 2009 biotech investment refers to investment in the cohort of biotech firms under observation in this study.

investments. A mere five spin-offs from Elan have attracted 65% of all venture capital investments, more than twice as much venture capital funding as twenty-one HEI spin-offs over the period in question[49]. Non-Elan private spin-offs and other private start-ups have each accounted for a mere 2% of venture capital funding, despite accounting for 31% of Irish biotech firms and 44% of Irish biotech employment. This is in keeping with Klepper's (2008) hypothesis that start-up companies are characterised by low competence, reflecting a lack of organisational and industry experience.

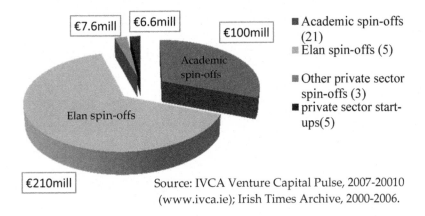

Source: IVCA Venture Capital Pulse, 2007-20010
(www.ivca.ie); Irish Times Archive, 2000-2006.

Figure 10.3: Irish Biotech Venture Capital Funding, 2000-2010

Note: Number of companies given in brackets; figures given in current values.

Table 10.2 provides a firm-level breakdown of these venture capital trends. Of the ten most successful Irish biotech firms in terms of attracting venture capital, five are Elan spin-offs. The data actually understates the extent of the relative success of the Elan spin-offs because some of these spin-offs raised a large part of their venture

---

[49] Our findings appear to be at variance with the findings of Munari and Toschi (2011). In the context of the micro- and nanotechnology sector in the UK, this study found no evidence of a venture capital bias against investment in academic spin-offs. Apart from the different sectoral context, the contrasting results may also stem from the indicators applied. In Munari and Toschi (2011), the ability of spin-offs to attract venture capital is measured by the incidence of venture capital investment, irrespective of the size of the investment. However, in our study, ability to attract venture capital is measured by the size of the actual investment.

capital prior to 2007 and/or have raised substantial funds as part of the initial public offering (IPO) process.

For example, Amarin had raised substantial private sector funding, prior to securing €70 million venture capital funding in 2009. AGI Therapeutics raised €9.5 million venture capital in 2004 and went on to raise a further €42.5 million in an IPO in Dublin and London in 2006. Azur Pharma was founded with private equity funding of $60 million in 2007 and the same year the company raised a further $50 million. Merrion Pharmaceuticals attracted €11 million venture capital in the first two years of operation, a further €21 million during the period 2007-2010 as well as €5.6 million at the time of the IPO.

Table 10.2: Firm-Level Breakdown of Venture Capital Flows, 2000-2010

Firm	Origins	€'000	Total €'000 (%)
Private sector spin-offs from Elan			210,320 (65%)
Amarin	Elan	85,900	
Azur	Elan	75,000	
Merrion pharma	Elan	33,500	
AGI	Elan	9,500	
Sigmoid Biotechnologies	Elan	6,420	
Other Private sector spin-offs			7,600 (2%)
Beocare (spin-off from Beocare Corp.)	Beocare Corp.	5,200	
Argutus Medical (spin-off from Biotrin)	Biotrin	1,500	
Neurocure (spin-off from BMR)	BMR	900	
HEI spin-offs			100,371 (31%)
Ntera (spin- off from UCD)	HEI (UCD)	28,000	
Biancamed	HEI (UCD)	7,550	
Biosensia	HEI (UCD)	3,900	
Celtic Catalysts	HEI (UCD)	1,711	
Bioobservation	HEI (UCD)	120	
Opsona Therapeutics	HEI (TCD)	22,900	
Cellix	HEI (TCD)	2,400	
Pharmatrin	HEI (TCD)	1,500	
Genable	HEI (TCD)	1,100	
Allegro (Deerac)	HEI (TCD)	800	

Identigen	HEI (TCD)	500
Sensl Technologies	HEI (UCC)	6,445
Hibergen	HEI (UCC)	5,500
Luxcel Biosciences	HEI (UCC)	3,000
Alimentary Health	HEI (UCC)	1,300
Luxcel	HEI (UCC)	100
Eirzyme	HEI (NUIG)	10,000
Crescent Diagnostics	HEI (UL)	1,045
Stokes Bio	HEI (UL)	1,000
Marvao	HEI (GMIT)	850
Neutekbio	HEI (DCU)	650
Private sector start-ups		6,600 (2%)
Topchem		2,500
Vysera		2,200
Aerogen		750
Megazyme		650
Eirgen		500

Source: IVCA *Venture Capital Pulse,* 2007-20010 (www.ivca.ie);
Irish Times Archive, 2000-2006.

Discussion and Conclusions

In this chapter, we have explored the extent to which Klepper's theory of spin-offs applies to the Irish biotechnology industry. Specifically, we assess whether or not entry by private sector and HEI spin-offs explains the evolution of the Irish biotechnology sector. We find that the growth of the Irish biotech industry over the last two decades has been shaped by two distinct forces: (i) spin-offs from Elan, a private sector firm which grew rapidly and then underwent significant corporate restructuring in 2002; and (ii) the emergence of enhanced HEI research capabilities in the biotechnology sector resulting from a systematic programme of investment in research in biotechnology and systematic attempts to commercialise this research through HEI spin-offs. The co-existence of these two distinct industry catalysts, which appear to have been largely independent of one another, suggests that the development of the Irish biotech industry must be understood in terms of two separate spin-off processes.

As per Klepper (2008), we find that a high competence parent (Elan) has borne high competence spin-offs, as indicated by the flow of venture capital in the industry. We show that in the attraction of investment funding, spin-offs from Ireland's most successful indigenous biotech firm, Elan, have enjoyed a superior performance relative to the spin-offs that emerged from Irish universities and relative to private sector start-ups. As noted above, for example, for the period 2000-2010 five Elan spin-offs attracted twice as much venture capital funding as the twenty-one HEI spin-offs in receipt of venture capital over this same period.

As discussed above, Elan itself can be considered to be, in the Klepper (2008) terminology, a high competence spin-off, as the founder left a parent company based in the United States, established his own company in an Irish location with few (if any) existing entrants, went on to become an industry leader, and in time spun off new high competence firms. This role played by inventor mobility as an important conduit for technological spill-overs has been documented by Almeida and Kogut (1990) and Breschi and Lissoni (2002). Without wishing to draw comparisons between the Irish biotech industry and other far more established industrial concentrations, we note that Klepper (2010) identifies a similar initiation process in both Detroit's automobile industry and Silicon Valley's integrated circuits industry. Indeed both Klepper (2008) and Buenstorf and Klepper (2009) point to the US automobile and tyre industries, respectively, as illustrations of how one firm can have a profound influence on the evolution of the geographic structure of an entire industry, in that it can catalyse the industrial concentration of that industry around a particular location.

A number of policy implications arise from our study of the Irish biotech industry, both of relevance to the Irish case and of broader application. The evolution of the Irish biotech industry serves as a reminder of the important role of divestment and corporate restructuring for new firm formation. The sudden divestment of biotechnology assets and product rights by an industry leader (Elan) has acted as the catalyst for the creation of a wave of high competence spin-offs, which have given new impetus to the Irish biotech industry. Similar processes have been identified in relation to the Information Technology industry (Barry and van Egeraat, 2008).

The formative role of private sector spin-offs in industry evolution suggests that policymakers should at least pay as much attention to stimulating private sector spin-offs as to HEI spin-offs, and should be mindful of the proportion of industrial promotion agencies' resources that are directed to each of these cohorts. At the same time, we are not saying that investment in the science base and the promotion of HEI spin-offs is necessarily counterproductive. Our findings have identified a number of success stories in this field. Rather, we are arguing for a greater focus on the commercial aspects of innovation in the science and industrial development promotion efforts of the state and its development agencies.

The broader implication for policy of our research is that government and government agencies should leverage the role of private sector spin-off processes and, within that, the role of high competence parents. However, this raises an age-old question for policymakers: is it possible to create high competence parents which will seed the development of new industries or should the focus be on creating the conditions in which high competence parents may emerge of their own accord?

Chapter 11
Irish Industrial Policy and Economic Clusters – An Analysis of The Green Way[50] (Dublin's Cleantech Cluster)

Deiric Ó Broin and David Jacobson

Introduction

This chapter[51] situates the debate about industrial policy, and in particular the notion of local industrial policy and the fostering of industrial clusters, in the context of three distinct but overlapping dynamics:

- The debate about the appropriate role for the state in the development of Ireland's economy;
- The crises recently – and to some extent still being - experienced by Ireland[52];
- The ongoing reform of Ireland's local government system.

In doing so it examines the relative paucity of robust public discourse regarding appropriate policy interventions in the economy and the lessons that can be drawn from one of the state's more recent innovations in local industrial policy. The purpose of this chapter, while addressing definitions of industrial policy and the various aspects of industrial policy, is to focus on how The Green Way relates to other components of Irish industrial policy and whether the spatial level at which it operates and the institutional environment that

---

[50] The Green Way has merged with the Green International Financial Services Centre (Green IFSC) to form Sustainable Nation Ireland, www.sustainablenation.ie.

[51] Earlier iterations and specific components of the chapter were presented at the Political Studies Association of Ireland (PSAI) Annual Conference in Dublin October 2013, the Irish Congress of Trade Unions Annual Conference in Dublin in April 2014, the Association of European Schools of Planning (AESOP) Annual Conference in Utrecht in July 2014 and the TASC Commission on Industrial Policy (2013-2014). The authors are grateful for the feedback from colleagues.

[52] The book uses the term 'crises' rather than 'crisis' because of the multi-stranded and separate nature of the economic, political and regulatory challenges facing Ireland (see Chapter 1 and Ó Riain, 2014:4-5).

facilitates its development provide lessons for other potential industrial policy initiatives at local level.

The chapter has a number of components. Section one outlines a working definition of industrial policy and details the reasons that this exercise is not as straightforward as one might think. Section two examines the complex nature of the debate around industrial policy and reviews a number of important elements of the discourse on industrial policy, including the link to tax policy, the role of MNCs, and the system of innovation in Ireland. Section three reviews the international evidence on local clusters and industrial policy and section four presents the experience of The Green Way, an initiative the authors view as an innovative industrial policy intervention at local level. The chapter concludes with a number of broad recommendations for local governments, including executive staff and elected councillors, and relevant regional and national agencies.

What is 'Industrial Policy'?
Up to the mid-1980s industrial policy (IP) was generally understood to refer to the direct intervention of the state, both in relation to production in general but also in relation to support for particular industries. Johnson's (1984:8) definition makes this clear: "Industrial policy means the initiation and coordination of governmental activities to leverage upward the productivity and competitiveness of the whole economy and of particular industries in it". Such industrial policy included elements of what had become a pejorative term for infant industry support, namely 'protectionism'. Import duties and quantitative import restrictions on certain goods were the most important of these elements. Others, like Harrop (1989), saw industrial policy as most appropriately excluding this kind of specific intervention and defined it as a creation of conditions – an economic environment – allowing business to flourish. This latter definition was inherent in the "Washington Consensus" that has been the dominant system of thinking about economics since the end of the 1970s. As we shall see, these two perspectives on what should constitute IP remain; directly interventionist on one hand and influencing only the environment of business on the other.

There had always been – and for developing countries there still is (Chang, 2003; Turok, 2007; Fine, 2013) – some backing for the idea that the state in late-industrialising countries might have to support certain industries in order to catch up to more developed economies. In the 1980s a substantial revision occurred to what had been the accepted wisdom in international economic theory and this provided further support for industry or sector-specific support. Krugman, 2008 Nobel prize-winner in Economics, proved that economies of scale and product differentiation were key factors – sometimes more important than the traditional comparative advantage, based on costs of production – in determining international competitiveness (e.g. Krugman, 1987). This led to what came to be called 'strategic trade policy' which was really the use of trade policy to encourage the development of particular sectors or sub-sectors, and not that different from what had previously been called 'industrial policy', at least in the way that for example Johnson (1984) understood that term. To illustrate, included in strategic trade policy would be the policy of the EU to support Airbus, and America's policy, in turn, to support Boeing. It could not be called industrial policy because, as Stiglitz (another Nobel prize-winner in Economics) and his co-authors have written, the market fundamentalism of the Washington Consensus made industrial policy "bad words not to be spoken either in public or in private by respectable people" (Cimoli *et al.*, 2009:1).

More recently Mazzucato (2013) has gone even further, unhesitant in her use of such bad words as "entrepreneurial state". She shows that the state is a key producer of innovation, not just through policy to influence company behaviour, but also directly through state-owned organisations like the National Institutes of Health in the US and the Medical Research Council in the UK. She also shows how the success of many of the giant companies – including Google and Apple – in the current phase of the information and communication technology (ICT) revolution, is built on state funding. Both policy and practice by the state have been essential in removing the risk and uncertainty that in many cases constitute insurmountable hurdles to private investment.

There is much other evidence and argument that alternatives to the neo-classical underpinnings of the Washington Consensus can provide a better basis for an understanding of IP. Pitelis (2006:435) shows this, providing a very broad definition – "a set of measures taken by a government and aiming at influencing a country's industrial performance towards a desired objective". He also argues that the direction of change in EU industrial policy is appropriately more consistent with evolutionary, rather than neo-classical, economics. He acknowledges the problem of differentiating between industrial, technology, regional and other policies and suggests that identification rest on what governments themselves define as their industrial policies. In an elaboration of his earlier discussion, Pitelis (2015:18) defines "developmental industrial policy" (DIP) as going beyond IP, "in that it involves purposive strategic intent, planning, and actions by the public sector to shape, extend, create, and co-create markets and ecosystems, as opposed to merely setting the 'rules of the game' (institutional framework), or focusing on solving 'market failures'. Cimoli *et al.* (2009:2) more narrowly define IP as including infant industry support, "trade policies, science and technology policies, public procurement, policies affecting foreign direct investments, intellectual property rights, and the allocation of financial resources". As Coates (2015:57) argues, "More focused industrial policy is back in vogue".

It is interesting to note that despite this broad re-acceptance in recent years of more interventionist IP, there remain differences among those in favour of such IP. This is clear, for example, from Mazzucato's (2013) emphasis on state support for high tech R&D in contrast to the economic geographers' emphasis on economies of agglomeration. In addition, there is a continuation of influential argument against interventionist IP. Thus Chang (2016:1), while calling for more detailed analysis of the results of SME (small and medium enterprise) policy in Korea, seems to accept that the essential objective of policy is to "correct market failures". We have already shown that Pitelis wants DIP to go beyond solving market failures. DIPs, he argues (2015:18), "can even often create 'market failures', so as to foster a wider developmental perspective".

In the Irish context, the first step in an analysis of IP must be an examination and categorisation of policies in terms of their impact on industry, broadly defined. This is so because, firstly, there is some doubt about whether there is such a thing as industrial policy in Ireland. There is a DIP, and has been since the end of the 1950s, with little change to its central plank. This, the heart of the Irish strategy for development is, and has been for half a century, to encourage inward foreign direct investment. The state agency in the pursuit of this policy is the Industrial Development Authority (IDA). There is also an agency with responsibility for implementation of policies supporting locally owned firms, Enterprise Ireland (EI), and a number of government projects and policies for example the various National Development

Plans, the annual Action Plans for Jobs, and Action Plan for Jobs "Disruptive Reforms". But there is little evidence that all these, and all other elements mentioned above, fit together with strategic consistency. That they all affect how industry (broadly defined to include business services) develops, there can be no doubt; so in this new, expansive view of what constitutes IP, Ireland definitely has one.

The very fact that such a range of policies exists in Ireland suggests a need for assessing and evaluating them as a totality. The approach of Stiglitz and his colleagues (in Cimoli *et al.*, 2009), like that of Pitelis (2006), builds on the evolutionary approach, asserting that the "accumulation of knowledge and capabilities, at the levels of both individuals and organizations" are essential to the emergence into sustainable development (Cimoli *et al.*, 2009:2).

For the purposes of this chapter, the first task is to show that there is an industrial policy in Ireland and to identify a variety of aspects of that policy. This will involve pinpointing the role and relevance of both policies and organizations. It should be emphasised, however, that given the scale of the task, the chapter that follows does no more than review certain aspects of industrial policy in Ireland, its primary focus is on the potential offered by coherent strategic policy interventions at local level[53]. Given the evidence presented here of lack of strategic coherence, there is a need for a major study of policy for economic development in Ireland, across all sectors. This is all the more essential now in the aftermath of the crises, the consequences of which were exacerbated by the structural excesses of the construction and banking sectors.

Industrial Policy is Complex

A critical issue in any debate about industrial policy is grasping the complexity of the area and the difficulties involved in providing simple or easy to implement recommendations. Any robust intervention must take account of:

---

[53] It is also worth noting the very idea of industrial policy has been politically problematic in much of the developed world. It has been called the "most controversial policy of our time" (Chang, 2003:7). Despite having a very significant number of policy tools available to policy makers there has been a clear and marked reluctance to acknowledge that the state implements an industrial policy. That we implement a poorly co-ordinated, and at times conflicting industrial policy, is a matter of academic debate, but the substantive matter that the state is implementing an industrial policy is the subject of considerable political reticence.

- The important role institutions play;
- State investment in industrial support;
- The role of tax policy;
- The position of MNCs in relation to the existing industrial policy of the state;
- The structure and functioning of the existing innovation system.

The analysis of these linked issues raises serious questions about how the state's existing industrial policy operates and suggests key areas where improvement may be achievable[54].

Institutions

A first approach is provided by Sean Ó Riain (2013), whose work on states and markets in industrial development, in general (2000; 2004a) and in Ireland (2004b; 2013), have provided a framework for a constructive critique of industrial policy. He shows that a whole variety of other policies impact on industry and that industrial policy itself is thus multi-faceted. Policies, agencies and institutions in such areas as education, skill development, innovation and research could and perhaps should be seen in terms of how they relate to industrial development.

Providing a particular interpretation of recent economic development in Ireland, Ó Riain provides evidence of the sustained impact of government on development, not just in Ireland but in such unlikely stalwarts of market-based societies as the United States. He points out, for example, that federal government laboratories are important providers of technological innovations. Other federal funding contributes to R&D and to inter-firm networks.

On the basis of this focus, he argues that in two areas in particular there is potential for the state in Ireland to contribute to an improvement in the prospects of the Irish economy, in research and innovation and among non-exporting firms. In relation to the first, state expenditure on research and innovation increased sharply during the late 1990s. The question is whether this expenditure was effective, whether it contributed to an increase in the innovativeness of Irish

---

[54] There now follow summaries of some of the key chapters in TASC's Commission on Industrial Policy, published as *The Nuts and Bolts of Innovation: New Perspectives on Irish Industrial Policy* (Jacobson 2013).

economy and society. Ó Riain (2013) suggests that the way this question is approached in Ireland is inappropriate. Rather than focusing only on whether and how research contributes to new products and processes, on the direct commercialisation of the results of research, we should be concerned with the broader question of the system of innovation, including the institutional mechanisms through which people, public organisations and firms interact in the formation and application of innovative capabilities to the development of firms. A remaining issue, raised by Ó Riain (2013) and awaiting comprehensive research, is the processes through which innovation is generated, applied and diffused in the system of innovation in Ireland.

A second area in relation to which Ó Riain (2013) has suggestions, is that of non-exporting, mainly indigenous firms. These include low and medium-tech firms, in manufacturing and services, that supply local consumers and both local and exporting businesses. The emphasis of the industrial support agencies on exporting firms, he shows, leaves relatively unaided the import-competing firms. They can be, and in many cases are already, important elements in inter-firm networks that may include exporting firms; a more integrated perspective on the development of a competitive Irish economy is therefore essential. Some evidence of the relevance of these topics for Ireland can be found in Heanue and Jacobson (2002; 2008). They are raised and analysed in some detail for other countries in Europe and beyond in two recent books, Hirsch-Kreinsen and Jacobson (2008) and Robertson and Jacobson (2011). Key issues arising for Irish industrial policy are how to identify potentially successful non-exporting indigenous firms, how to support them and, if and when they do become successful, what policy should be towards acquisition of them by foreign companies.

One element of state support for indigenous firms in Ireland is funding. Ó Riain (2013) argues that there are weaknesses in the patterns of organisational capability in the banking system. These make it unlikely that, even after the worst of the financial crisis is behind us, the banks will be able to perform the function of financing development of indigenous firms that is required. There is a case, therefore, for a state investment bank to co-ordinate the integration of various agencies' support schemes with the raising of finance from the private sector.

State Expenditure on Industry Support

While Ó Riain addresses the complexity of industrial policy through the institutional context, Paul Sweeney (2013) shows that if industrial policy is understood in terms of all government activity that impacts on firms, then another approach is to follow the money. Sweeney's previous work has focused on state-owned companies (Sweeney, 1990; 2004) and, more broadly, on the explanations for and limits of Ireland's Celtic Tiger successes (Sweeney, 1998; 2008). His recent work (2013) examines in some detail expenditure out of the public purse that has an impact, directly and indirectly, on enterprise sector activities. What this shows, among other things, is that taxpayers contribute euros in the order of hundreds of millions to the enterprise sector in Ireland. This funding by the taxpayer of businesses of various kinds and in all sectors is both direct, in the form of grants and subsidies, and indirect, through the budgets of agencies like Enterprise Ireland and the Industrial Development Authority. Sweeney (2013) also addresses the issue of tax expenditure, where taxes are foregone in an attempt to provide incentives to investors to create jobs.

A clear example of such tax expenditure aimed at creating jobs is provided in the reduction of income taxes for high paid executives of multinational companies (MNCs) in the first 2012 budget. Thirty per cent of their salaries of up to €500,000, were made exempt from income tax. There was a proposal prior to the next (December 2012) budget to increase the Universal Social Charge (USC) for high earners. This was rejected, according to the head of the IDA, because "not increasing the USC on top earners was necessary for Ireland to remain competitive in attracting foreign direct investment (FDI)"[55]. Over and above not increasing the USC, the Minister for Jobs, Enterprise and Innovation, Richard Bruton, proposed a further reduction in the income tax of highly paid executives of foreign companies, claiming that this would result in more subsidiaries of MNCs setting up in Ireland, and more jobs being created as a result[56]. The Minister for Finance, Michael Noonan, decided not to incorporate the proposal into his budget. From an equity perspective, this decision is obviously positive; even leaving aside the question of how many – or few! – jobs might have been created by this tax expenditure, it would have been an extremely

---

[55] Ronan McGreevy, "Bruton says Budget won't be changed", *The Irish Times*, 7th December, 2012.

[56] Carl O'Brien, "Bruton sought multinational tax breaks", *The Irish Times*, 7th May, 2013.

problematic signal for all those facing reduced wages and increased taxation in the context of the Troika bailout budgets. From the perspective of industrial policy, the key issue here is the absence of analytical argument, based on empirical evidence, that this tax expenditure would indeed have had a net impact on job creation.

Sweeney's (2013) work provides many other examples of both direct and indirect subsidies to private enterprise. He makes clear that, as with the example of reduction of income tax for the benefit of MNC executives, the impact of many of these is not known, not calculated and not sought. The decisions on the tax expenditures and other elements of policy that together make up broad industrial policy are based to a greater extent on politics than economics.

Corporate Taxes and Industrial Policy

It is already clear from the above that there is a relationship between tax policy and industrial policy. The sustained effort of the Minister for Jobs, Enterprise and Innovation, Richard Bruton, to reduce income tax levels for high paid executives of MNCs[57], reflects the focus on encouraging foreign direct investment (FDI) as the main plank of industrial policy. Many other policies, including income tax rates, are seen as secondary to, and having to be tailored for, the policy of incentivising FDI.

Jim Stewart has long been among the main analysts of fiscal policy and FDI and has contributed much to an understanding for example of profit switching transfer pricing (Stewart, 1989). More recently he has focused, among others, on policy for enterprise development (2005). Recent work focuses directly on the question of the importance of the corporate tax rate to industrial policy in Ireland. There are a number of targets in his critical examination of corporate tax rates. First, there is the question of the rate itself and whether it is too low. This is not to accept that the nominal rate is the actual, or effective rate, and certainly for many companies the effective rate is much lower than the nominal rate. Moreover, the effective rate paid by many companies in other countries, even countries with high nominal rates, is also very low. Indeed, it can even be argued that we should have a higher rate so that we can encourage particular activities (like R&D) by offering "clawbacks" where there is expenditure on those activities.

---

[57] Pamela Newenham, "Bruton criticises high income tax rate", *The Irish Times*, 8th April, 2013.

The recent controversy surrounding the statement by American Senators Levin and McCain that Ireland is a tax haven – rejected by Irish Ambassador Michael Collins – addresses many of the issues raised in Stewart's (2013) recent work. What seems to be missed in the debate, but made clear by Stewart, is that it is not a question of corporate tax rates. Rather it is the regulatory fiction of companies operating in one jurisdiction, but being liable for taxes in another jurisdiction. How this is done is generally through MNCs having a multitude of identities, those in the lowest tax regimes declaring the greatest profits.

What Stewart's work on corporate taxation in Ireland shows is that, as a result of the use of corporate tax regulation to encourage FDI, there is a huge amount of time, skill and effort expended in tax "consultancy". Much of this actually influences the tax system itself, because the key sources for information on how to change tax rules and regulations are the same organisations that advise MNCs – and others – on how to minimise tax payments. If this time, skill and effort were instead expended on development of indigenous firms, their products and services, the consequences would be far more positive for the growth of the Irish economy. Corporate tax policy is a key element in Irish industrial policy, but it emerges from Stewart's work that the particular set of policies and regulations around corporate taxation in Ireland is a relatively ineffective, and certainly inappropriate, means of achieving industrial development.

The System of Innovation

The literature on Ireland's system of innovation provides a number of indications of possible strengths and weaknesses, both in what policy focuses on, and in the capabilities of the system. There is little doubt that in Ireland – as in many other countries (Hirsch-Kreinsen and Jacobson, 2008; Robertson and Jacobson, 2011) – there has been an over-emphasis in policy on high-tech innovation. This is not to say that high-tech innovation is not important, but that innovation incorporates a great deal more than, for example, patents emanating from advanced scientific research. A firm, district, region or economy that is productive in terms of patents, is not necessarily successful, whether success is measured by profits, growth, exports or even survival. Even firms that undertake R&D frequently produce non-research-based innovations to a greater extent than patents (Arundel and Robertson,

2012). The dynamic capability of firms, districts regions and economies is a far more important characteristic than the ability to produce patents, though of course the two are not mutually exclusive. Dynamic capability is more important because it is the ability to create new, and access existing knowledge, and to apply it in new ways or in new combinations. It includes the ability to identify whether existing or new knowledge is necessary. It is thus more comprehensive, a higher order capability, than the ability to undertake R&D. Arguably, by finding ways through policy of enhancing dynamic capability, we would do more than improve R&D; we would generate the ability to distinguish between the need for R&D and the need for other, non-research-intensive ways of innovating. By so doing, we would enhance efficiency in the production of all innovation.

In relation to existing efficiency in the system of innovation in Ireland, recent research (Jacobson, 2013) provides very tentative evidence that Ireland is in some sense better at producing non-R&D-based innovation than R&D-based innovation. There is a great deal more work to be done in this area, for example using the complete data set from the EU's Community Innovation Survey. However, if these tentative findings are borne out by subsequent research, the policy implications are that more innovation would be generated by euros supporting other innovation-producing activities than by euros supporting R&D.

The inadequacy in both data on and analysis of different policies and projects supporting innovation is also pointed out by Jacobson (2013). Improvement in this area would also facilitate better decision making in relation to expenditure of the scarce funding for innovation in Ireland. In addition to questions on the types of innovation being supported, some attention also must be focused on the types of firms receiving support for innovation. Jacobson (2013) raises questions associated with industrial and business service sectors and sub-sectors, but size of firm and whether it is Irish or foreign owned, and whether it is part of a local or international cluster, are also relevant for future research.

MNCs and Irish Firms: Export Performance

As is already clear, MNCs are a fundamental element in Irish industrial policy. The question of the extent to which industrial policy should rely on foreign investment goes back at least to the discussions on the policy regime to replace protectionism in the 1950s. The Department of Industry and Commerce, for example, while supporting the tax incentives to encourage foreign investment, also insisted on maintaining elements of the Control of Manufactures Acts on the grounds that complete repeal of these acts "...would permit of the unfettered investment of outside capital in unsuitable as well as suitable cases" (quoted in Barry and Daly, 2011:166)[58].

Apart from political economy issues of governance and the location of power and control, economic behaviour and performance differences between MNCs and Irish-owned firms are important in industrial policy. For the years up to the end of the 1970s these have all been the subject of comprehensive review by Eoin O'Malley for the National Economic and Social Council (O'Malley, 1980). More recently he contributed to a paper on the characteristics and performance of indigenous and foreign firms in Ireland (Barry, Bradley and O'Malley, 1999). He has also focused on competitiveness (O'Malley, 2004:2013).

O'Malley (2004) shows that contrary to the view that Ireland's Celtic Tiger performance of the 1990s was the result primarily of the growth of the foreign-owned sectors, many indigenous sectors also experienced faster growth in output, employment and exports than their competitors in the EU. Rather than in terms of relative costs, O'Malley (2013) defines competitiveness in terms of ability to compete in open markets. The evidence, when it is measured in this way, is that Ireland actually gained in competitiveness over the period 2000 to 2008, with greater gains more recently. There are some significant differences, within this overall positive picture, between manufacturing and services, and between foreign-owned and indigenous sectors. In manufacturing, in relation to foreign and indigenous firms in particular, the data indicate that Irish firms' improvement in competitiveness began from 2005 while that of MNCs began later, in 2008. This diversity underlines the argument against a focus on national price and wage data as a means of determining whether or not the Irish economy is competitive. Overall, his research calls for a much more careful examination of the factors generating competitiveness than the usual focus on wage costs alone.

It follows from even such a surface review of issues in industrial policy addressed in this chapter that Ireland has an industrial policy.

---

[58] The question of local vs foreign ownership had already been raised in relation to the first MNC in Ireland, the Ford motor company (Jacobson, 1977).

Among the aspects of this industrial policy addressed here are policies on MNCs, on corporate taxation, on public expenditure, on R&D and innovation, and on environmental protection. What is clear is that there is a disconnect, in the sense that these different aspects of industrial policy are frequently not seen as relating to one another. There is at least a potential for tension between policies supporting foreign direct investment and rigorous environmental protection. Given the differences between MNC and Irish firms' export performance, policies to support industrial (and service sector) development must be amenable to subtle distinction. Given the vast amounts being spent in public expenditure on enterprise support of various kinds, a clear analysis of the net effect of these different kinds of support is essential. The next sections of the chapter review previous international efforts to foster industrial clusters and the recent experience of The Green Way in Dublin.

International Efforts to Foster Industrial Clusters

Rosenfeld (2002) provides a helpful framework for evaluating efforts to foster industrial clusters. In his work for the Directorate General for Regional Policy and Cohesion of the European Commission he identified a number of key ingredients of successful local industrial policy aimed at fostering cluster development. These include:

- Establishing and/or recognising cluster organisations;
- Facilitating external linkages;
- Encouraging cluster communications channels;
- Developing human capital;
- Including social equity as an aim;
- Successfully directing investment towards cluster R&D.

Rosenfeld's analysis suggests that these characteristics tend to be present in successful initiatives because they address the critical barriers facing underperforming local and regional economies:

> Various historic under-investments limit clusters in less favoured regions from gaining new, or holding onto existing, competitive advantages. Most can be traced to a weak infrastructure; lack of access to technology, innovation, and capital; regional insularity and

isolation; low educational levels and low skilled work force; absence of talent; and an overly mature or hierarchical industry structure. Social exclusion exists in places with large and isolated underprivileged and undereducated populations; technological exclusion exists in places with poor access to sources of technology and benchmark companies; and economic exclusion is a result of weak links to benchmark regions and markets (2002:9).

Recent research by the OECD builds on Rosenfeld's work and details a number of the critical issues facing policy makers and how they can be addressed (Potter *et al.*, 2012). They note the important role played by policy in the emergence of cleantech clusters in Sweden, Denmark, and California, USA. In each of these cases, the emergence of the cleantech cluster was driven by the meeting of "strange attractors" at path inter-dependent crossroads, which subsequently mutated into cluster-platforms of related variety industry. This occurred despite differences in their national and regional political and economic contexts.

In every case illustrated, cleantech clusters emerged from something else and combined capabilities from diverse industries – from agro-engineering to wind turbines, from pulp and paper to organic cotton, and algae biofuels to ICT and biotechnology.

How can policy foster such developments? Potter *et al.* (2012:34-35) contend that there are two major points. The first point is that policy has a role to play in facilitating the collaboration among cluster firms that can lead to innovation. It can achieve this by offering three benefits to firms and other agents that actively comply with the new designation of cluster member. All of them are to be seen openly in the Swedish "co-ordinated market" model.

New Cluster Members
The first is to have the opportunity of meeting new members in their own market segment, or more importantly, different but related market segments to exploit the known innovation and development potential from recombinant knowledge across industry interfaces. This also includes "the prospect of forming relationships with larger customer firms seeking to strengthen innovation networks and supply chains" (Potter *et al.*, 2012:34).

Transversality

Second, the "transversality" initiatives underpinning the development of the embryonic Sustainable Business Hub and Training Regions clusters in Sweden were induced by the offer of incentives to companies for participation in innovation projects. Transversality occurs where clusters are seen as modules to be integrated with different clusters to generate innovations and meet higher goals. The incentives take the form of medium-term innovation projects involving teams displaying "difference but compatibility" (Ibid.).

An output of this induced transversality is "green packaging", which brings together food companies (in fact organic food firms) that cannot be affordably serviced by large firms such as Tetrapak but who seek a packaged branding that shows they are organic and act sustainably. A more technical example relates to milk packaging, which requires perfect sealing from its "bioplastic" (starch-based) packaging. This has been developed through exploitation of nanotechnology expertise from the new materials cluster. The transversal initiatives supporting the development of cleantech clusters in Sweden have also been facilitated by subsidised cluster management teams, which promote collaboration and broker joint innovation projects across cluster firms.

Access to Other Clusters

The final incentive that cluster members receive for participating in clean-tech cluster programmes is access to other clusters in different as well as similar industries. This affords a spreading of good practice knowledge of technological and developmental business paradigms elsewhere, including abroad, and experience of what, in support terms, may work in one place or industry while being unknown elsewhere. Such advantages would not come easily through market engagement alone.

The second lesson for policy makers is that in the best cases cleantech cluster emergence is a product of a political process in which learning occurs on the upper and lower levels of the multi-level governance system, involving both national and local policy makers. The OECD refer to Västra Götaland in Sweden as an excellent example of "the implementation of a regional green strategy" (2012:5) from the beginning of the 2000s involving the integration of the European

Union's "Gothenburg Model of the Lisbon Strategy" into its regional development strategy. The learning can also occur in the opposite direction, from regional to national level. California was long used to its state anti-pollution policies being templates for later federal regulations as embodied in various Clean Air Acts. In Denmark "active concertation between regional industry groupings and national ministries has produced generations of useful regulation and incentive that helped reinforce the regional cleantech clusters" (Potter *et al.*, 2012: 36).

The Green Way[59] – Dublin's Cleantech Cluster

Irish policymakers' interest in the concept of industrial clusters dates back to the Culliton Report, which recommended the promotion of industrial clusters focused on niches of national competitive advantage. This view of agglomeration economies based on industrial clusters derives largely from the work of Michael Porter (1990). The Culliton report elicited widespread agreement that Ireland should seek to develop clusters of deep competitive advantage. Culliton's central policy recommendation was that a network programme was a valuable first step towards this development. The term network refers to a group of firms, with restricted membership, who agree to co-operate in certain activities for a mutual gain.

A follow-up report by NESC argued that Irish development policy should move from state responsibility and state provision to a partnership approach. Irish policy in a number of areas - macro-management, local development and long-term unemployment - has been moving in this direction in recent years. The proposed network programme would reinforce this trend. Irish industrial policy initiatives which incorporated a cluster development component include:

- Strategic Research Clusters;
- Centres for Science, Engineering and Technology;
- Competence Centres;
- Technology Transfer Offices;
- Industry-Led Networks Pilot Programme;

---

[59] The Green Way has merged with the Green International Financial Services Centre (Green IFSC) to form Sustainable Nation Ireland, www.sustainablenation.ie.

- Innovation Partnerships;
- Applied Research Enhancement (Institute of Technologies);
- Skillnets;
- Fusion (ITI).

In this rich and diverse range of initiatives a number of stakeholders in North Dublin have developed and implemented what might best be termed as a number of place-linked industrial policy initiatives (Peck, Connolly, Durnin and Jackson, 2013). The stakeholders include Dublin City Council, Dublin City University, Fingal County Council, Dublin Airport Authority and a number of smaller organisations including the North Dublin Chamber of Commerce and the local development agencies operating in the region. These initiatives included:

- Task Force on Knowledge-based Development (2002);
- Developing Sustainable Industrial Clusters in North Dublin (Jacobson and McGrath, 2004; Willams and Shiels, 2004; McGrath, 2008);
- Accelerated Skills Development Programme (Logan and Ó Broin, 2004);
- North Dublin Venture Capital Fund (2006).

The Green Way follows in a similar manner and brings together many of the same partners. It was established in early 2010 as *An tSlí Ghlas - The Green Way*, aiming to be a green economic corridor stretching from Dublin's city centre along a north-city spine via Ballymun to Dublin Airport, and potentially much further afield. It was initially established as an entrant into the internet-based 'Your Country, Your Call' competition, an initiative led by Martin McAleese (RTÉ, 2010).

From its establishment The Green Way, conscious of the complex political climate it operated in, portrayed itself as Dublin's cleantech cluster, focused on "attracting inward investment, supporting indigenous firms and creating a world-class centre of excellence" (Ernst and Young, 2012:42). In this regard it proved very successful and consolidated its position as "a good example of a project building on Ireland's R&D expertise in the cleantech space to attract foreign investment" (Ernst and Young, 2012:29).

In what follows, the work of Rosenfeld (2002), the OECD (2012 and 2013) and Hilliard and Jacobson (2013) is used to map and review The Green Way's development.

Institutional Capacity

Rosenfeld (2002:10) observes that clusters depend on social institutions for "a variety of things they cannot do internally or get from other companies". Successful clusters use such institutions for "information about and help with advances in technologies, economic scans, brokering, and education and training at all levels in their industries". The Green Way stakeholders quickly established a legal entity and staff complement to drive the initiative. This entity was, in turn, quickly recognised by key government departments and relevant public agencies. The critical issue becomes what assets and resources the cluster organisation is able to leverage from its relationships. Clusters are defined by relationships. Ultimately, they are self-selecting based on how individual employers and institutions in a region "define their missions, set their priorities, use their region's resources, and form relationships" (Rosenfeld, 2002:6). In the case of The Green Way the relationships were initially and predominantly with public institutions. The leadership of each of the key public institutions displayed considerable commitment to the initiative and senior staff from all of the public institutions engaged in a variety of considered and resource intensive ways. In addition the SME representatives through the North Dublin Chamber made very significant contributions to the work of The Green Way and a number of Chamber representatives were given considerable leeway for their employers to work with The Green Way in its establishment phase. Unfortunately this was neither sufficient nor sustainable in the medium term. This will be discussed in more detail below.

Facilitating External Linkages

The Green Way was accepted as a member of the Global Cleantech Cluster Alliance[60] (GCCA) in November 2010 and hosted the GCCA

---

[60] The Global Cleantech Cluster Association is a non-profit association that creates conduits for companies to harness the tremendous benefits of international cleantech cluster collaboration in an efficient, affordable, and structured way. Global cleantech provides a gateway for established and emerging Cleantech companies to gain exposure

Awards in Dublin in 2011. In addition, the Green Way actively engaged with EcoCluP[61], the European equivalent. Furthermore, The Green Way, building on its links with DCU and DIT, developed a series of strategic links with the key enterprise support and economic development agencies, the IDA and Enterprise Ireland.

Encouraging Cluster Communications Channels

Communications proved to be quite problematic. Davies (2013:1290) observes that "the cleantech sector in Ireland is characterised by a small number of large players (e.g. Intel and Siemens) and a large number of SMEs, a few of which are considered highly innovative with strong international growth potential". As a result the ability of The Green Way to meaningfully contribute to intra-sector communications was constrained. For many SMEs their primary communications link was with Enterprise Ireland and possibly a research link with a university or institute of technology. Such SMEs rarely engaged with local business networks, e.g. Chambers of Commerce, and MNCs such as Intel or Siemens were much more likely to communicate directly to the IDA and central government while having a research relationship with a university or institute of technology.

Facilitating Collaboration among Cluster Firms that can lead to Innovation

As noted above clusters can offer three benefits to firms:

- The opportunity to meet new members in their own market segment, or more importantly, different but related market segments;
- Incentives for companies to participation in innovation projects;
- Access to other clusters in different as well as similar industries.

---

to potential investors, new markets, influential networks, innovative technologies and best practices.

[61] EcoCluP is the first pan-European partnership of cluster organisations focusing on the eco-innovative industries. The partnership represents most of Europe's key clusters with a strong environmental portfolio with cluster organisations participating from Austria, Denmark, Finland, France, Germany, Hungary, Ireland, the Netherlands, Spain, Sweden and the UK. The overarching goal of the EcoClup project is 'to adapt, test, validate, and implement services and tools supporting the growth and internationalisation of eco-innovative companies organised in environmental clusters across Europe.

A key constraint hampering the success of The Green Way relates to the nature and stage of development of the cleantech sector in Ireland. Both Davies (2013) and Ernst and Young (2012) note that despite the success of other technological sectors in Ireland, the cleantech sector did not receive similar levels of "attention, focus and support" (2013:1290). In addition the "weakly developed green procurement policy" of large public agencies was identified by SME representatives, in particular, as a critical barrier to expansion of the sector. From the North Dublin Chamber of Commerce's perspective it was very difficult to advocate the economic logic of cleantech and work to persuade member SMEs to examine the potential offered by the sector when the largest purchasers of products and services, i.e. government and public agencies, had a very poorly thought through approach to such matters. In addition the decision to centralize many public procurement activities through the Office of Government Procurement made it increasingly difficult for SMEs to engage with public procurement contracts (Flynn, Davis, McKevitt and McEvoy, 2012; Flynn and Davis, 2015).

The Green Way was constrained in its ability to incentivise company participation in innovation projects. This relates to its limited funding and to, a significant extent, the perception by companies that they should be grant-aided to do it. Newman (2014:242-243) notes the considerable history of grant support to the manufacturing sector in Ireland and it is important to note that many SMEs and MNCs continue to attract significant support from public agencies for a variety of activities. As a result there is an expectation that there will be some inducement or incentive to engage in the type of activity The Green Way was attempting to encourage.

However, there were considerable successes. For example, The Green Way successfully drew down funding for SMEs through its involvement in Climate-KIC, the EU's main climate innovation initiative[62], and funding through Enterprise Ireland to develop a Living

---

[62] Climate KIC (Knowledge Innovation Community) is part of the European Institute of Innovation and Technology (EIT), with a mandate to enhance Europe's ability to innovate in the low-carbon sectors. Climate-KIC is one of Europe's largest public-private innovation partnerships focused on climate change. It integrates education, entrepreneurship and innovation resulting in connected, creative transformation of knowledge and ideas into economically viable products or services that help to mitigate climate change. This activity has represented Ireland's first formal relationship with EIT-KICs. Through participation in Climate KIC, both The Green Way and Energy Cork secured, for 2015, almost €290,000 in direct support for Irish organisations innovating in

Lab programme, essentially test-beds for clean technologies, services and processes across a number of targeted themes.

Linked to this was the expectation that research and development resources of the founding higher education institutions would be freely available, or at a nominal cost, to be utilised. This was a source of considerable confusion for many SMEs. There was little appreciation of the considerable costs borne by higher education institutions and the limited capacity to engage in projects without appropriate external funding.

In relation to member companies' access to clusters in different as well as similar industries, a critical constraint was the lack of organisations similar to The Green Way. As a result the type of cluster-to-cluster interaction one might expect wasn't possible. Consequently the "offer" to potential members of the cluster was restricted in comparison to some of its counterparts in the EU.

Industry Leadership

The authors previously noted that institutional capacity in a region is a critical success factor for cluster establishment and consolidation. In the case of The Green Way the public institutions and the SME representative organisation, the North Dublin Chamber, worked very closely together to establish and drive the work of the cluster. However, a substantial body of evidence suggests that "behind every successful cluster is a group of innovative firms led by people, who value learning, are committed to their community and, therefore, are willing to work toward a collective vision for their industry" (Rosenfeld, 2002:9). These leading companies may have a niche or rapidly growing market that is not threatened by competition, or may face such intense global competition that the benefits of mutual support and learning outweigh concerns about confidentiality (Rosenfeld, 2007). The "key to building and sustaining a cluster organisation often rests with the support of these benchmark companies" (Rosenfeld, 2002:9). Unfortunately the establishment of The Green Way coincided with economic and financial crises in Ireland and many of the leading companies one would expect to take early stage leadership positions in the work of The Green Way did not become involved. This contrasts

---

the low-carbon sector. Funding up to 100% will be available to participants to facilitate a series of education, training, incubation and entrepreneurship programmes for practitioners involved in the low carbon sector.

with the Copenhagen Cleantech Cluster where significant commercial stakeholders, e.g. Dong and Vestas, were involved from the outset, or Stryia in Austria where a new cluster organisation was developed from existing industrial networks and led by key industry leaders (MacNeill and Steiner, 2010; Temouri, 2013).

Regulatory Environment

Hilliard and Jacobson (2013) provide evidence for the Irish context to support an earlier argument by Porter and Van der Linde (1995) that rigorous environmental protection can improve competitiveness. They also show that enterprise development is important for innovation and should therefore be a focus of industrial policy. There is a close analogy between the dynamic capability that firms require for responding to improved environment protection regulation, and the dynamic capability that firms require for innovation in general. And innovation in this context should include new forms of inter-firm relationships. A consequence of all this for the analysis of the Green Way may be that if the environmental regulation were more rigorously inspected and implemented, and if the dynamic capabilities of the organisations involved had been better developed, the project would have been more successful. A green criterion in procurement is an example of the former, and innovative forms of training for inter-firm/inter-organisational networking an example of the latter.

Conclusion

Industrial policy in Ireland has a complex and at times contested lineage. The role of the state in fostering economic development has been relatively successful, though the evidence suggests that some of the instruments employed often undermine the effectiveness of others. The recent work of Ó Riain (2013), Stewart (2013), Jacobson (2013), O'Malley (2013) and Hilliard and Jacobson (2013) details the complexity that arises in this context. The role of local government is, in some ways, even more problematic for a number of reasons:

- Local government in Ireland tends to be under-researched (Kirby, 2008);
- The type and nature of economic development the local state has engaged in has tended to be related to property, e.g. working with

the IDA to develop sites for MNCs or the building and management of enterprise centres with Enterprise Ireland;

- The policy instruments available to local governments are limited;
- The importance of economic development as a core competence of local government is relatively recent and the legal and policy framework is still being established, e.g. the drafting and implementation of the new City and County Local Economic and Community Development Plans;
- The localness of innovative economic activity tends to remain unappreciated by national policy makers; place is important.

In this context the authors believe that policy makers, industry leaders and political representatives can learn a great deal from the experience of The Green Way. It came to fruition in a time of crises and in a gap in the national policy framework. It was an innovative partnership and achieved considerable success. Furthermore, its failings were not of its making, but reflect problems with national-level approaches to local economic development. For example, one of the consequences of using a low corporation tax rate as an instrument of industrial policy is that a culture of expectation develops among companies, both SMEs and MNCs. This undermines efforts to develop jointly funded partnerships between public, private and civil society stakeholders.

The experience of The Green Way suggests that a considerable number of challenges face Irish local governments when working to nurture clusters. These challenges primarily relate to place-sensitivity, building capacity, improving institutional knowledge and managing relationships with other key institutions, e.g. universities.

To a certain extent local governments are already responding to these challenges and the opportunities provided by the recent legislative reforms. Economic development is being institutionally recognised as a key area of activity. This is a welcome development and bodes well for the future. Furthermore, the need for greater place-sensitivity in Irish industrial policy and consideration of the role that local governments should play in the design as well as delivery of national and local economic strategies appears to have been addressed. The legislative and public policy framework has been put in place to facilitate such an approach but it will be some time before it is clear how successful this has been.

With regard to improving institutional knowledge, Rosenfeld refers to a need to be able to formulate and implement "unconventional public policy" (2007:20), policies that shift the focus of attention from an individual place or individual firm to a region and clusters of businesses. In this regard it is important that local governments learn how businesses interact and how clusters work. As noted above clusters are driven by relationships, not just their constitutive elements. Building this tacit knowledge base inside local governments is vital. There are significant constraints, including the employment embargo and the organisational culture of mobility between policy areas and subsequent promotional prospects for generalists. However, international evidence (e.g. UK and Canada) suggests that the recognition of economic development as a professional area/discipline will improve the capacity of local governments.

The final challenge for local governments relates to managing relationships; previous research by the authors (Ó Broin and Jacobson, 2010) suggests that such relationships tend to be based on individuals rather than organisations. There has been considerable improvement since then and The Green Way is an example of one type of institutional partnership of which there is more successful evidence in other countries. An explicit incorporation of the importance of sustainability into industrial policy formulation (see Aiginger, 2015) would certainly enhance the likelihood of building sustainable local economies in Ireland.

APPENDIX I
MEMBERSHIP OF THE LORD MAYOR'S TASK FORCE ON VACANT LAND LEVY

Chairperson: Oisín Quinn, Lord Mayor of Dublin

Danny McCoy, CEO, Irish Business and Employers Confederation

David Begg, General Secretary, Irish Congress of Trade Unions

Frances Ruane, Director, Economic and Social Research Institute

Tom Dunne, Head of School of Real Estate and Construction Economics, DIT

Killian O'Higgins, Chartered Surveyor

Derek Tynan, DTA Architects

Brendan Williams, lecturer in Urban Development and Urban Economics, UCD

David Brennan, CEO Dublin City Business Association

Micheál Collins, Senior Research Officer, Nevin Economic Research Institute

Councillor Mary Freehill, Chair of the Economic Development, Planning and International Relations Strategic Policy Committee, Dublin City Council

Councillor Ruairi McGinley, Dublin City Council

Philip Maguire, Acting Dublin City Manager

Kathy Quinn, Head of Finance, Dublin City Council

Peter Finnegan, Director, Office of Economy and International Relations, Dublin City Council DCC

Jim Keogan, Assistant City Manager, Planning and Economic Development,

Ali Grehan, Dublin City Architect

Kieran Rose, Senior Planner, Dublin City Council

Paul Kearns, Senior Executive Planner, Dublin City Council

APPENDIX II
DERELICT SITES ACT 1990

The Derelict Sites Act 1990 allows a local authority to take action in relation to a site that is 'derelict' within the term of the Act. Landowners, who do not comply with a notice to carry out certain specified improvement works, can be levied 3% of the market value of the land.

However not all vacant land would come within the legal definition of 'derelict', hence there is a gap in the legal infrastructure.

Section 3 of the Act sets out the following:

3.—In this section *"derelict site"* means any land (in this section referred to as *"the land in question"*) which detracts, or is likely to detract, to a material degree from the amenity, character or appearance of land in the neighbourhood of the land in question because of—

(*a*) the existence on the land in question of structures which are in a ruinous, derelict or dangerous condition, or

(*b*) the neglected, unsightly or objectionable condition of the land or any structures on the land in question, or

(*c*) the presence, deposit or collection on the land in question of any litter, rubbish, debris or waste, except where the presence, deposit or collection of such litter, rubbish, debris or waste results from the exercise of a right conferred by statute or by common law.

APPENDIX III
LOCAL GOVERNMENT BUSINESS IMPROVEMENT DISTRICTS ACT 2006

129B.— (1) Subject to and in accordance with this Part, the rating authority for an administrative area may by resolution—

(a) specify an area within the administrative area and establish that area as a business improvement district, and

(b) approve implementation of a scheme ('BID scheme') to carry out or provide one or more projects, services or works described in subsection (2) and which scheme is financed in whole or in part by BID contribution levies under this Part.

REFERENCES

A

Abel, R.J., Dey, I., Gabe, T.M. 2012. "Productivity and the Density of Human Capital", *Journal of Regional Science*, 52(4): 562-586.

Adshead, M., and Quinn, B. 1998. "The Move from Government to Governance: Irish Development Policy's Paradigm Shift", *Policy and Politics*, Vol. 26, No. 2, 209–225.

Ahlstrom, D. 2010. "Remedy to Close Gap between Stem-Cell Research and Human Trial". *The Irish Times*, 11th November, 2010.

Aiginger, K. 2015. "Industrial Policy for a Sustainable Growth Path". New Perspectives on Industrial Policy for a Modern Britain, Bailey, Cowling and Tomlinson. eds. Oxford: Oxford University Press.

Almeida, P. and Kogut, B. 1990."Localization of Knowledge and the Mobility of Engineers in Regional Networks". *Management Science*, 45, 905-917.

Allan, P. 2003. "Why Smaller Councils Make Sense". *Australian Journal of Public Administration*, Vol. 62, No. 3, 74-81.

Andrews, R. 2010. "Organizational structure and public service performance", in *Public Management and Performance: Research Directions*, Walker, R.M., Boyne, G.A., and Brewer, G.A., eds., Cambridge: Cambridge University Press, 89-109.

Andrews, R., and Boyne, G. 2012 "Structural Change and Public Service Performance: The Impact of the Reorganization Process in English Local Government", in *Public Administration*, Vol. 90, No. 2, 297-312.

Arundel, A. and Robertson, P.L. 2012. "R&D and Other Sources of Knowledge in Open Innovation", Unpublished Working Paper, Australian Innovation Research Centre, University of Tasmania.

Asheim, B., Boschma, R., and Cooke, P. 2011. "Constructing regional advantage: platform policies based on related variety and differentiated knowledge bases", *Regional Studies*, 45(7), 893-904.

Asheim B., Cooke, P., and Martin, R. 2006. "The rise of the cluster concept in regional analysis and policy: a critical assessment", in *Clusters and Regional Development: Critical reflections and explorations*, Asheim, B., Cooke, P., and Martin, R. eds., Routledge, London, 1-19.

B

Bailey, D., Cowling, K., and Tomlinson, P.R. eds. 2015. *New Perspectives on Industrial Policy for a Modern Britain*, Oxford: Oxford University Press.

Baldersheim, H., and Rose, L.E. 2010. "A Comparative Analysis of Territorial Choice in Europe – Conclusions", in *Territorial Choice: The Politics of Boundaries and Borders*, Baldersheim, H., and Rose, L.E., eds., Basingstoke: Palgrave Macmillan, 234-259.

Barrington Report. 1991. *Local Government Reorganisation and Reform: Report of the Advisory Expert Committee*, Dublin: Stationery Office.

Barry, F., Bradley, J., and O'Malley, E. 1999. "Indigenous and Foreign Industry: Characteristics and Performance", in *Understanding Ireland's Economic Growth*, Barry, ed., Macmillan, UK.

Barry, F., and Daly, M.E. 2011. "Mr. Whitaker and Industry: Setting the Record Straight", *Economic and Social Review*, Vol. 42, No. 2, 159-168.

Barry, F., and Van Egeraat, C. 2008. The Decline of the Computer Hardware Sector: how Ireland Adjusted, *ESRI Quarterly Economic Commentary*, Spring 2008, 38-57.

Berube, A., Friedhoff, S., and Nadeau, C. 2010. *Global Metro Monitor The Path to Global Recovery*, The Brookings Institution, Washington.

Birch, D. 1979. "The Job Generation Process", Cambridge MA: US Department of Commerce, MIT Program on Neighborhood and Regional Change.

Bish, Robert L. 2001. "Local Government Amalgamations: Discredited Nineteenth-Century Ideals Alive in the Twenty-First", C.D. Howe Institute Commentary – The Urban Papers, no. 150 http://cdhowe.org/sites/default/files/attachments/research_papers/mixed/bish.pdf (Accessed January, 2017).

Blöchliger, H., and Campos, J.P. 2011. "Tax Competition Between Sub-Central Governments", OECD Working Papers on Fiscal Federalism, No. 13, Brussels: OECD Publishing.

Blom-Hansen, J. 2010. "Municipal Amalgamation and Common Pool Problems: The Danish Local Government Reform in 2007", in *Scandinavian Political Studies*, Vol. 33, No. 1, 51-73.

Boschma, R.A., and Frenken, K. 2011. The Emerging Empirics of Evolutionary Economic Geography in *Journal of Economic Geography* 11, 295-307.

Boschma, R.A., and Wenting, R. 2007. "The Spatial Evolution of the British Automobile Industry: Does Location Matter?"in *Industrial and Corporate Change*, 16 (1).

Boyne, G. 1995. "Population Size and Economies of Scale in Local Government", in *Policy and Politics*, Vol. 23, No. 3, 213-222.

Breschi S., and Lissoni, F. 2002 "Mobility and Social Networks: Localized Knowledge Spillovers Revisited". CESPRI Working Paper, No. 142.

Brink, J., McKelvey, M., and Dahlander, L. 2004. "The Dynamics of Regional Specialisation in Modern Biotechnology" in *The Economic Dynamics of Modern Biotechnology*, Laage-Hellman, J., McKelvey, M., and Rickne, A. eds. Edward Elgar Publishing. Cheltenham.

Buckley, D. 2013. "Development land prices triple in less than a year". *The Sunday Business Post*. 27th October, 2013.

Buenstorf, G., and Klepper, S. 2009. Heritage and Agglomeration: the Akron Tyre Revisited in *Economic Journal*, 119, 705-733.

Butler, S. 1981. *Enterprise Zones: Greenlining the inner-cities*. London: Heinemann Educational.

Byrnes, J., and Dollery, B. 2002. "Do Economies of Scale Exist in Australian Local Government? A Review of the Research Evidence", in *Urban Policy and Research*, Vol. 20, No. 4, 391-414.

C

Callan, T., Keane, C., Savage., M., and Walsh, J. 2012. *Analysis of Property Tax Options – A Report to the Interdepartmental Expert Group on Property Tax*, Dublin: Economic and Social Research Institute.

Callanan, M., and Keogan, J. 2003. *Local Government in Ireland: Inside Out*, Dublin: IPA.

Callanan, M. 2007. "Continuity and adaptation in local government", in *Recycling the State: The Politics of Adaptation in Ireland*. Hayward, K., and MacCarthaigh, M. eds. Dublin: Irish Academic Press, 133-153.

Callanan, M., and MacCarthaigh, M. 2008. 'Local Government Reforms in Ireland', in *Local Government Reform: A Comparative Analysis of Advanced Anglo-American Countries*. Dollery, B.E., Garcea, J., and LeSage Jr. E. C. eds., Cheltenham: Edward Elgar, 104-132.

Callanan, M., Murphy, R., and Quinlivan, A. 2012 "Myths and Realities of Economies of Scale in Local Government", Paper presented to the Regional Studies Association and Political Studies Association of

Ireland Symposium on 'Local Government Reform: Myth or Reality?', NUI Maynooth, 8th March, 2012.

CDLR (Steering Committee on Local and Regional Authorities). 1995. The size of municipalities, efficiency and citizen participation, Local and Regional Authorities in Europe, no. 56, Strasbourg: Council of Europe.

CDLR (European Committee on Local and Regional Democracy). 2001. Relationship Between the Size of Local and Regional Authorities and their Effectiveness and Economy of their Action, Report by the CDLR, Strasbourg: Council of Europe.

Central Statistics Office. 2011. *This is Ireland: Highlights from Census 2011, Part 1*, Dublin: Stationary Office.

Central Statistics Office .2012. *Business in Ireland 2010*. Dublin: Stationery Office.

Chang, H-J. 2003. *Globalisation, Economic Development and the Role of the State*. Zed Books, London.

Cimoli, M., Dosi, G., and Stiglitz, J.E. 2009. "The Political Economy of Capabilities Accumulation: The Past and Future of Policies for Industrial Development", in *Industrial Policy and Development: The Political Economy of Capabilities Accumulation*, Cimoli,M., Dosi, G., and Stiglitz, J.E. eds. Oxford University Press, Oxford.

City and County Managers' Association. 2012a. "Interim Report to the Minister of the Environment, Community and Local Government and the LGER IG", Appendix 1: Financial performance and savings of the local authority sector 2008-2012. Available at http://www.housing.gov.ie/sites/default/files/migrated-files/en/Publications/LocalGovernment/Administration/FileDownLoad,33712,en.pdf (Accessed 20th November, 2013).

City and County Managers' Association. 2012b. "Local Authority Support to Enterprise and Business: Analysis of Economic Templates – Report to the County and City Managers' Association Enterprise Strategy Steering Group". Available at http://www.lgma.ie/sites/default/files/newsfiles/ccma_report_on_local_authority_support_to_enterprise_and_business.pdf (Accessed 10th March, 2016).

City and County Managers' Association. 2013. "Supporting Enterprise, Local Development and Economic Growth: Analysis of Local Authority Activities for 2012". Available at http://www.lgma.ie/en/supporting-enterprise-local-development-

and-economic-growth-analysis-local-authority-activities-2012. (Accessed 10th March, 2016).

Clarke, G. ed. 2008. *Towards Open Cities*, Madrid: British Council.

Clarke, S. 1982. "Enterprise Zones: Seeking the Neighbourhood Nexus", in *Urban Affairs Quarterly*, 18:53-71.

Coates, D. 2015. "Industrial Policy: International Experiences" in *New Perspectives on Industrial Policy for a Modern Britain*, Bailey, Cowling and Tomlinson. eds. Oxford: Oxford University Press.

Collins, M., and Larragy, A. 2011. *A Site Value Tax for Ireland: Approach, Design and Implementation*. Trinity Economic Working Paper No. 1911, Dublin: Trinity College Dublin.

Collins, J. 2012. "Free Public Wi-Fi; A Capital Idea?", *The Irish Times*, 12th January, 2012.

Commission on Taxation. 1985. *Fourth Report of the Commission on Taxation: Special Taxation*, Dublin: Government Publications Office.

Commission on Taxation. 2009. *Report of the Commission on Taxation*, Dublin: Stationery Office.

Communities and Local Government. 2011. *Enterprise Zone Prospectus*. London: Department of Communities and Local Government.

Connolly, N. "Labour seeks to tax unused land and boost development". *The Sunday Business Post*. 11th August, 2013.

Connolly,N. "CIF attacks Labour plan for levy on vacant development sites". *The Sunday Business Post*, 8th September, 2013.

Conservative Party. 2009. *Control Shirt: Returning power to local communities*. Policy Green Paper No. 9. London: Conservative Party.

Conservative Party. 2010a. *Open Source Planning*. Policy Green Paper No. 14. London: Conservative Party.

Conservative Party. 2010b. *Big Society, Not Big Government*. Conservative Party: London.

Convery, F. 2013. "Property Tax – Why Dubliners Should Pay More". Available at PublicPolicy.ie http://www.publicpolicy.ie/property-tax-why-dubliners-should-pay-more. (Accessed 21st November, 2013).

Council of European Municipalities and Regions. 2011. *Dexia and CEMR publish 2010-2011 edition of Key Figures on Local and Regional Europe*. Available at http://www.ccre.org/docs/ANG_Press_Release_key_figures_local_and_regional_European_figures.pdf. (Accessed 14th March, 2017).

Cooke, P. 2001. Regional Innovation Systems, Clusters, and the Knowledge Economy, in *Industrial and Corporate Change*, 10, 4, 945-974.

Creative Dublin Alliance. 2012. *A Road Map for Branding Dublin*. Dublin: Dublin City Council.

Cullingworth, B., and Nadin, V. 2006. *Town and Country Planning in the UK*. 14th ed. Oxon: Routledge.

Culliton Report. 1992. *A Time for Change: Industrial Policy for the 1990s, Report of the Industrial Review Group*. Dublin: Stationery Office.

D

Daly, M. E. 2001. "The County in Irish History" in *County & Town: One Hundred Years of Local Government in Ireland*, Daly, M.E. ed. RTÉ Thomas Davis Lecture Series: Winter 1999. Dublin: Institute of Public Administration, 1-11.

Daly G. 2008. "Azur Pharma loss of $7.2m despite huge revenue surge", *The Post*, 23rd November, 2008.

Davies, A.R. 2013. "Cleantech Clusters: Transformational Assemblages for a Just, Green Economy or just Business as Usual?" in *Global Environmental Change*, 23(5): 1285–1295.

Davis, S. J., Haltiwanger, J.C., and Schuh, S. 1996a. *Job Creation and Destruction*, Cambridge: MIT Press.

Davis, S. J., Haltiwanger, J.C., and Schuh, S. 1996b, *Small Business and Job Creation: Dissecting the Myth and Reassessing the Facts*, Working Paper No. 4492, Cambridge: National Bureau of Economic Research.

Department of Finance. 2010a. *EU/IMF Programme of Financial Support for Ireland*, Dublin: Government Publications Office

Department of Finance. 2010b. *Report of the Tax Strategy Group 2010*. Dublin: Government Publications Office.

Department of Public Expenditure & Reform. 2012. *Comprehensive Expenditure Report 2012-2014*, Dublin: Government Publications Office.

Devlin Report. 1969. *Report of the Public Services Organisation Review Group*, Dublin: Stationery Office.

Dollery, B., and Fleming, E., 2005. "A Conceptual Note on Scale Economies, Size Economies and Scope Economies in Australian Local Government", Working Paper 2005-6, Working Paper Series in Economics, University of New England. Available at http://www.une.edu.au/bepp/working-papers/economics/1999-2007/index.php. (Accessed 10th March, 2017).

Dowding, K., John, P., and Biggs, S. 1994. "Tiebout: A Survey of the Empirical Literature", in *Urban Studies*, Vol. 31, Nos. 4/5, 767-797.

Drennan, J. 2011. "The Joy of Cuts – Perfect Bedtime Reading for us All', *Sunday Independent*, 31st July, 2011.

Dublin City Council. 2008. "Funding the Dublin City Region", Dublin: Dublin City Council Publication.

Dublin City Council. 2012. "Adopted Budget 2012". Available at http://www.dublincity.ie/YourCouncil/AbouttheCouncil/CouncilSpendingRevenue/Documents/Adopted_RevenueBudget_2012_Web.pdf. (Accessed 2nd June, 2013).

Dublin Local Authorities. 2009. *Economic Action Plan for the Dublin City Region*, Dublin: Dublin City Council.

Dunne, T. 2005. "Land Value Taxation: Persuasive Theory but Practically Difficult", *Property Valuer*, IAVI, Dublin, Ireland, (Spring 2005).

E

Edquist, C. 2005. Systems of Innovation – Perspectives and Challenges in *The Oxford Handbook of Innovation*. Fagerberg, J., Mowery, D.C., and Nelson, R.R. eds., Oxford: Oxford University Press.

Ernst and Young. 2012. *Cleantech Ireland*, Dublin: Ernst and Young.

European Commission, Community Directorate for Regional Policy. 2007. *State of European Cities – Adding Value to European Urban Audit*, Brussels: European Commission.

European Commission. 2010. *Establishment of a National Asset Management Agency: Asset Relief Scheme for Banks in Ireland*. Brussels: European Commission.

EVCA .2010. *EVCA Yearbook 2010*, Brussels: European Private Equity and Venture Capital Association.

F

Fine, B. 2013. "Beyond the Developmental State: An Introduction" in *Beyond the Developmental State: Industrial Policy into the 21st Century*. Fine, B., Saraswati, J., and Tavasci, D. eds. London: Pluto, 1-32.

Foroohar, R. 2016. *Makers and Takers, The Rise of Finance and the Fall of American Business*. Penguin Random House.

Flynn, A., Davis, P., McKevitt, D., and McEvoy, E. 2012. "Sustainable Public Procurement in Practice: Case Study Evidence from Ireland" in *Charting a Course in Public Procurement Innovation and Knowledge Sharing*, Albano, G.L., Snider, K.F., and Thai, K.V. eds. Florida: PrAcademic Press, 150-173.

Flynn, A., and Davis, P. 2015. "The rhetoric and reality of SME-friendly procurement" in *Public Money and Management*, 35 (2): 111-118.

Fox, W.F., and Gurley, T. 2006. "Will Consolidation Improve Sub-National Governments?", World Bank Policy Research Working Paper 3913, 2006/05. Available at http://econ.worldbank.org. (Accessed 10th March, 2017).

G

Geoghegan W. and Pontikakis, D. 2008. "From Ivory Tower to Factory Floor? How Universities are Changing to Meet the Needs of Industry", in *Science and Public Policy*, 35(7) 462-474.

Glenn A., Glossop, C., Harrison, B., Nathan, M., and Webber, C. 2007. "Innovation and the City". NESTA.

Goldstein, D., Hilliard, R., and Parker, V. 2011. "Environmental Performance and Practice across Sectors: Methodology and Preliminary Results", *Journal of Cleaner Production*, Vol. 19, No. 9, 946-957.

Gorman W., and Cooney, T. 2007. "An Anthology of Enterprise Policy in Ireland", *Irish Journal of Management*, Vol. 28, Issue 2, 1–28.

Government of Ireland. 1971. *Local Government Reorganisation – White Paper*, Dublin: Stationery Office.

Government of Ireland. 1991. *Local Government Reorganisation and Reform*, Dublin: The Stationery Office.

Government of Ireland. 1993. *Industial Development Act, 1993*. Dublin: The Stationery Office.

Government of Ireland. 1996. *Better Local Government – A Programme for Change*, Dublin: Stationery Office.

Government of Ireland. 2008. *Green Paper on Local Government: Stronger Local Democracy – Options for Change*, Dublin: Stationery Office.

Government of Ireland. 2009. *Report of the Special Group on Public Service Numbers and Expenditure Programmes*, Dublin: Government Publications Office.

Government of Ireland. 2010. *Report of Local Government Efficiency Review Group*, Dublin: Government Publications Office.

Government of Ireland. 2012. *Putting People First: Action Programme for Effective Local Government*, Dublin: Stationery Office.

Government of Ireland. 2013. *Supporting Economic Recovery and Jobs – Locally: Local Government Sectoral Strategy to Promote Employment and Support Local Enterprise*, Dublin: Stationery Office.

Grist, B. 2011. "Politicians and the Irish Planning Process: Political culture and impediments to a strategic approach", *Journal of Irish and Scottish Studies*, 4 (2):159-172.

Gunn, H. D. 1991. Local Government's Role in Retaining Capital for Community Economic Development available at http://sustainable-city.org/articles/capital.htm. (Accessed January, 2015).

Gurdgiev, C. 2009. "Macroeconomic Case for a Land Value Tax Reform in Ireland", Smart Taxes Network, Policy Paper available at https://papers.ssrn.com/sol3/papers.cfm?abstract_id=2029519. (Accessed 10th March, 2017).

H

Hanley, M., and O'Gorman, B. 2004. "Local Interpretation of National Micro-Enterprise Policy: To what Extent has it Impacted on Local Enterprise Development?" *International Journal of Entrepreneurial Behaviours and Research*, Vol 10, No. 5, 305–324.

Harrison, F. 2005. *Boom Bust*, London: Shepheard-Walwyn Ltd.

Harrop, J. 1989. *The Political Economy of Integration in the European Community*, Cheltenham: Edward Elgar.

Hayward, K. 2010. "Divide to Multiply: Irish Regionalism and the European Union" in Europe, *Regions and European Regionalism*, Scully, R. and Wyn Jones, R. eds. Basingstoke: Palgrave Macmillan, 90-114.

Heanue, K., and Jacobson, D. 2002 "Organizational Proximity and Institutional Learning: The Evolution of a Spatially Dispersed Network in the Irish Furniture Industry", *International Studies of Management & Organization*, Vol.31, No.4, Winter 2001-2, 56-72.

Heanue, K., and Jacobson, D. 2008 "Embeddedness and Innovation in Low and Medium Tech Rural Enterprises", *Irish Geography*, Vol.41, No.1, 113-137.

Higher Education Authority. 2006. *Who Went to College in 2004?* Dublin: Higher Education Authority.

Hilliard, R., and Jacobson, D. 2003. "Organisational Capabilities and Environmental Regulation: The Case of the Pharmaceutical Sector in

Irish Regions," in *Irish Regional Development: A New Agenda*, O'Leary, E. ed. Dublin: The Liffey Press.

Hilliard, R., and Jacobson, D. 2011. "Cluster Versus Firm Specific Factors in the Development of Dynamic Capabilities in the Pharmaceutical Industry in Ireland: A Study of Responses to Changes in Environmental Protection Regulations", *Regional Studies*, Vol. 45, No. 10, 1319-1328.

Hilliard, R., and Jacobson, D. 2013. "Industrial Policy and Sustainability" in *The Nuts and Bolts of Innovation: New Perspectives on Irish Industrial Policy*, Jacobson. ed. Dublin: Glasnevin Publishing.

Hirsch-Kreinsen, H., and Jacobson, D. eds. 2008. *Innovation in Low-Tech Firms and Industries*, Cheltenham: Edward Elgar.

H.M. Treasury, Department of Trade and Industry and Office of the Deputy Prime Minister. 2006. *Devolving Decision Making: 3 - Meeting the Regional Economic Challenge – The Importance of Cities to Regional Growth*, London: HM Treasury.

Houlberg, K. 2010. "Municipal Size, Economy and Democracy" in *Territorial Consolidation Reforms in Europe, Swianiewicz, P. ed. Budapest: Local Government and Public Service Reform Initiative*, Open Society Institute, 309-331.

I

IDA Ireland. 2008. *Annual Report*, Dublin: IDA.

IDA Ireland. 2010. *Horizon 2020*, Dublin: IDA.

Indecon. 2005. *Review of Local Government Financing*, Dublin: Department of the Environment, Heritage and Local Government.

Indecon. 2008. *Review of County/City Development Board Strategic Reviews and Proposals for Strengthening and Developing the Boards*, Dublin: Department of Environment, Heritage and Local Government.

International Labour Office. 2012. *Cities With Jobs – Policy Paper 2012*. Available at http://www.ilo.org/employment/Whatwedo/ Publications/working-papers/WCMS_191502/lang--en/index.htm. (Accessed January, 2017).

International Labour Office. 2014. Boosting Local Economies Fact Sheet. Available at http://www.ilo.org/empent/Publication/WCMS _175521/lang--en/index.htm. (Accessed January, 2015).

J

Jacobson, D. 1977. "The Political Economy of Industrial Location: The Ford Motor Company at Cork 1912-1926", *Irish Economic and Social History*, Vol. 4, 36-55.

Jacobson, D. 2013. "Innovation Policy and Performance in Ireland" in *The Nuts and Bolts of Innovation: New Perspectives on Irish Industrial Policy*, Jacobson, D. ed. Dublin: Glasnevin Publishing.

Johnson, C. 1984. "The idea of industrial policy", in *The Industrial Policy Debate*, Johnson, C. ed. Institute for Contemporary Studies, San Francisco.

K

Keane, C., Walsh, J.R., Callan, T., and Savage, M. 2012. "Property Tax in Ireland: Key Choices", Renewal Series Paper 11. Dublin: The Economic and Social Research Institute.

Kearns, P., and Ruimy, M. 2010. *Redrawing Dublin*, Kinsale: Gandon Editions.

Kelly, O. 2013. "Everyone Stumps Up Cash Except Land Hoarders", *The Irish Times*, 5th August, 2013.

Kelly, O. 2013. "Developers may be Forced to Sell Vacant Sites", *The Irish Times*, 5th August, 2013.

Kelly, O. 2013. "OPW Targeted for Criticism over Vacant Sites", *The Irish Times*, 5th August, 2013.

Kelly O. 2013. "Planning Minister Jan O'Sullivan backs Mayor's Proposed Vacant Site Levy", *The Irish Times*, 19th August, 2013.

Kenny, L. 2003. "Local Government and Politics" in *Local Government in Ireland, Inside Out*, Callanan, M. and Keogan, Justin, F. eds. Dublin: Institute of Public Administration, 103-122.

Kirby, P. 2008. "Explaining Ireland's Development: Economic Growth with Weakening Welfare". Social Policy and Development Programme Working Paper Number 37. UNRISD. Available at http://www.unrisd.org/80256B3C005BCCF9/(httpPublications)/D359 85C0845ED8F3C12575120031778C. (Accessed 10th March, 2017).

Klepper, S. 2007. "Disagreements, Spin-Offs, and the Evolution of Detroit as the Capital of the US Automobile Industry", *Management Science*, 53(4): 616-631.

Klepper, S. 2008. *The Geography of Organizational Knowledge*. Pittsburgh: Mimeo, Carnegie Mellon University.

Klepper S. 2010. "The Origin and Growth of Industry Clusters: the Making of Silicon Valley and Detroit", *Journal of Urban Economics*, 67(1): 15-32.

Kuhlmann, S., and Wollmann, H. 2011. "The Evaluation of Institutional Reforms at Sub-national Government Levels: A Still Neglected Research Agenda", in *Local Government Studies*, 37(5): 479-494.

L

Laage-Hellman, J., McKelvey, M,. and Rickne, A. 2004. "Introduction" in *The Economic Dynamics of Modern Biotechnology*, Laage-Hellman, J., McKelvey, M., and Rickne, A. eds. Cheltenham: Edward Elgar Publishing.

Lassen-Dreyer, D., and Serritzlew, S. 2011 "Jurisdiction Size and Local Democracy: Evidence on Internal Political Efficacy from Large-Scale Municipal Reform", in *American Political Science Review*, 105(2): 238-258.

Local Government Efficiency Review Group. 2010. *Report of the Local Government Efficiency Review Group*, Dublin: Stationery Office.

Lundvall, B. 1992. *National Innovation Systems: Towards a Theory of Innovation and Interactive Learning*, London: Pinter.

Lyons, R. 2012. "Residential Site Value Tax in Ireland: An Analysis of Valuation, Implementation and Fiscal Outcomes". Available at: http://smarttaxes.org/wp-content/uploads/2012/01/Site-Value-Tax-in-Ireland-Identify-Consulting-final-report.pdf. (Accessed 10th March, 2017).

Lyons, W.E., and David Lowery. 1989. "Governmental Fragmentation Versus Consolidation: Five Public-Choice Myths about How to Create Informed, Involved, and Happy Citizens", in *Public Administration Review*, 49(6): 533-543.

M

Mac Cormaic, R. 2013. "Four Courts overhaul plan sets out vision for city-centre legal campus" *The Irish Times*, 29th August, 2013.

MacNeill, S., and Steiner, M. 2010. "Leadership of Cluster Policy: Lessons from the Austrian Province of Styria" in *Policy Studies*, 31(4):441-455.

Mahon, A.P., Faherty, M., and Keys, G.B. 2012. *Tribunal of Inquiry into Certain Planning Matters and Payments*, Dublin: Government Publications Office.

Malerba, F. 2003. "Sectoral Systems: How and Why innovation Differs Across Sectors", in *Handbook of Innovation*, Fagerber, J., Mowery, D., and Nelson, R., eds. Cambridge: Cambridge University Press.

Malo, S. and Norus, J. 2009. "Growth Dynamics of Dedicated Biotechnology Firms in Transition Economies. Evidence from the Baltic Countries and Poland", *Entrepreneurship & Regional Development*, 21(5 and 6): 481–502.

Marlow, D. 2011. "Enterprise Zones: Why They're Just a Distraction from the Cuts", *The Guardian*, 30th March, 2011.

Massey, D. 1982. "Enterprise Zones: a political issue." *International Journal of Urban and Regional Research*. 6(3):429-434.

Mayor, K., Lyons, S., and Tol, R. 2010. "Designing a Property Tax Without Property Values: Analysis in the Case of Ireland", paper Series 352. Dublin: Economic and Social Research Institute.

Mazzucato, M. 2013. *The Entrepreneurial State: Debunking Public vs Private Sector Myths*, London: Anthem Press.

McCarthy Report. 2009. *Report of the Special Group on Public Service Numbers and Expenditure Programmes*, Dublin: Stationery Office.

McDonald, F. 1985. *The Destruction of Dublin*, Dublin: Gill and Macmillan.

McDonald, F. 2000. *The Construction of Dublin*, Dublin: Eblana Editions.

McKinsey. 1971. *Strengthening the Local Government Service – A Report Prepared for the Minister for Local Government by McKinsey & Company, Inc.*, Dublin: Stationery Office.

Meyler, A., and Strobl, E. 2000. "Job Generation and Regional Industrial Policy in Ireland", *Economic and Social Review*, 31(2) 111–128.

Mieszkowski, P. 1972. "The Property Tax: An Excise Tax or a Profits Tax?" *Journal of Public Economics*, 1 (1): 73–96.

Millar, H. 2007. "Biotech's Defining Moments", *Trends in Biotechnology*, 25 (2), 56-59.

Mintzberg, H. 1983. *Structure in Fives: Designing Effective Organizations*, New Jersey: Prentice Hall.

Moore, B., and Potter, P. 2002 "Evaluation of the employment effects of United Kingdom Enterprise Zones: a comparison of new start-ups and inward investors" in *Regional Policies and Comparative Advantage*, Johansson, B., Karlsson, C., and Stough. R., eds. Cheltenham: Edward Elgar Publishing Limited.

Morgenroth, E. 2008. "Exploring the economic geography of Ireland", *Journal of the Statistical and Social Inquiry Society of Ireland*, 38:42-73.

Mouritzen, P.E. 1989. "City Size and Citizens' Satisfaction: Two Competing Theories Revisited', in *European Journal of Political Research*, 17(6): 661-688.

Mouritzen, P.E. 2010. "The Danish Revolution in Local Government: How and Why?" *Territorial Choice: The Politics of Boundaries and Borders*, Baldersheim, H., and Rose, L.E. eds. Basingstoke: Palgrave Macmillan, 21-41.

Moylan, K. 2011. *Irish Regional Policy: In Search of Coherence*, Dublin: Institute of Public Administration.

Munari F., and Toschi L. 2011. "Do Venture Capitalists Have a Bias Against Investment in Academic Spin-Offs? Evidence from the Micro- and Nanotechnology Sector in the UK" in *Industrial and Corporate Change*, 20(2): 397-432.

Myint, Y.M., Vyakarnam, S., and New, M., 2005. "The Effect of Social Capital in New Venture Creation: the Cambridge High-Technology Cluster" in *Journal of Strategic Change*, 14:165-177.

N

National Asset Management Agency .2009. *National Asset Management Agency Bill*. Available at: https://www.nama.ie/fileadmin /user_upload/NAMABill.pdf. (Accessed September, 2011).

National Asset Management Agency. 2010a. *Key Tranche 1 Data*. Dublin: NAMA

National Asset Management Agency. 2010b. *The National Asset Management Agency- A Brief Guide*. Dublin: NAMA.

National Asset Management Agency. 2011a. *Annual Report and Financial Statements 2011*. Dublin: NAMA.

National Asset Management Agency. 2011b. *NAMA Business Plan Version Two*. Dublin: NAMA.

National Asset Management Agency. 2012. *Annual Report and Financial Statements 2012*. Dublin: NAMA.

Namawinelake. 2012. NAMA Makes Major Concession to make its Accounts More Transparent. [Online] Available at https://namawinelake.wordpress.com/2012/01/23/nama-makes-major-concession-to-make-its-accounts-more-transparent. (Accessed November, 2012).

National Competitiveness Council. 2009. *Our Cities: Drivers of National Competitiveness*, Dublin: Forfás.

National Competitiveness Council. 2011a. *Statement on Competitiveness Priorities*, Dublin: Forfás.

National Competitiveness Council. 2011b. *The Cost of Doing Business in Ireland*, Dublin: Forfás.

National Treasury Management Agency . 2009. *Evaluation of Options for Resolving Property Loan Impairments and Associated Capital Adequacy of Irish Credit Institutions: Proposal for a National Asset Management Agency (NAMA) Abridged Summary of Report*. Dublin: NTMA

Nelson R., and Winter, S. 1982. *An Evolutionary Theory of Economic Change*, Cambridge MA: The Belknap Press.

NESC. 2004. *Housing in Ireland: Performance and Analysis*, Dublin: National Economic and Social Council.

Neumark, D., Wall, B., and Zhang, J. 2008. Do Small Businesses Create More Jobs? New Evidence from the National Establishment Time Series, Working Paper 13818, National Bureau of Economic Research, available at http://www.nber.org/papers/w13818. (Accessed 28th January, 2016).

Newman. C. 2014. "Manufacturing and Traded Services Sector" in *The Economy of Ireland: National and Sectoral Policy Issues*. O'Hagan, J., and Newman, C. eds. Dublin: Gill and Macmillan.

Newton, K. 1982. "Is Small Really so Beautiful? Is Big Really So Ugly? Size, Effectiveness, and Democracy in Local Government" in *Political Studies*, 30(2):190-206.

Nosella, A., Petroni, G., and Verbano, C. 2005. Characteristics of the Italian Biotechnology Industry and New Business Models: The Initial Results of an Empirical Study" in *Technovation*, 25(8):841–855.

O

Organisation for Economic Co-operation and Development. 1996. *Ireland: Local Partnerships and Social Innovation*, Paris: OECD Publishing.

Organisation for Economic Co-operation and Development. 2006a. *OECD Biotechnology Statistics*, Paris: OECD Publishing.

Organisation for Economic Co-operation and Development. 2006b, *Competitive Cities in the Global Economy, Territorial Review*, Paris: OECD Publishing.

Organisation for Economic Co-operation and Development. 2007. *Competitive Cities: A New Entrepreneurial Paradigm Shift in Spatial Development*, Paris: OECD Publishing.

Organisation for Economic Co-operation and Development. 2008. *OECD Public Management Reviews – Ireland: Towards an Integrated Public Service*, Paris: OECD Publishing

Office of Deputy Prime Minister. 2003. *Transferable Lessons from Enterprise Zones*, London: ODPM.

Orsenigo, L. 2001. "The (failed) Development of Biotechnology Cluster: the Case of Lombardy" in *Small Business Economics*, 17: 77–92.

Ó Broin, D., and Jacobson, D. eds. 2010. *Local Dublin, Global Dublin: Public Policy in an Evolving City Region*, Dublin: Glasnevin Publishing.

Ó Broin, D. 2010. "Governance Challenges in a Developing City Region', in *Local Dublin, Global Dublin: Public Policy in an Evolving City Region*, Ó Broin, D., and Jacobson, D. eds. Dublin: Dublin City University Press at Glasnevin Publishing, 180-198.

O'Hanlon, N. 2011. "Constructing a national house price index for Ireland" in *Journal of the Statistical and Social Inquiry Society of Ireland*, Volume 40: 167-196.

O'Malley, E. 1980. *Industrial Policy and Development: A Survey of Literature from the Early 1960s to the Present*, Dublin: NESC.

O'Malley, E. 2004. "Competitive Performance in Irish Industry" in *ESRI Quarterly Economic Commentary*, Winter: 66-101.

O'Malley, E. 2013. "Ireland's Competitive Performance" in *The Nuts and Bolts of Innovation: New Perspectives on Irish Industrial Policy*, Jacobson, D. ed. Dublin: Glasnevin Publishing.

Ó Riain, S. 2000. "States and Markets in an Era of Globalization" in *Annual Review of Sociology*, 26: 187-213.

Ó Riain, S. 2004a. *The Politics of High Tech Growth: Developmental Network States in the Global Economy*, Cambridge: Cambridge University Press.

Ó Riain, S. 2004b. "State, Competition and Industrial Change in Ireland 1991 – 1999" in *Economic and Social Review*, 35(1): 27-53.

Ó Riain, S. 2013. "Ireland's Industrial Policy Challenge" in *The Nuts and Bolts of Innovation: New Perspectives on Irish Industrial Policy*, Jacobson, D. ed. Dublin: Glasnevin Publishing.

Ó Riain, S. 2014. *The Rise and Fall of Ireland's Celtic Tiger: Liberalism, Boom and Bust*, Cambridge: Cambridge University Press.

Ó Riordáin, S. 2007. *Mapping Social Inclusion in Local Authorities*, Dublin: Combat Poverty Agency.

Ó Riordáin, S. 2015. "Placing local government at the heart of economic renewal", in *Local Governance, Development and Innovation*, Ó Broin, D. and Jacobson, D. eds. Dublin: Glasnevin Publishing.

P

PA Cambridge Economic Consultants. 1987. *An Evaluation of the Enterprise Zone Experiment*. London: HMSO.

PA Cambridge Economic Consultants. 1995. *Final Evaluation of Enterprise Zones*. London: HMSO

Papke, L. 1993. "What do we know about Enterprise Zones?" in *Tax Policy and Economy*, Volume 7, Poterba, J. ed. Cambridge, MA: MIT Press.

Pearson, P. 2001. *The Heart of Dublin: Resurgence of an Historic City*, Dublin: O' Brien Press.

Peck, F., Connolly, S., Durnin, J., and Jackson, K. 2013. "Prospects for 'place-based' industrial policy in England" in *Local Economy*, 28 (7) 828 – 841.

Pitelis, C.N. 2006. "Industrial Policy: Perspectives, Experience, Issues", in *International Handbook on Industrial Policy*, Bianchi, P., and Labory, S. eds. Cheltenham: Edward Elgar Publishing.

Pitelis, C.N. 2015. "DIP-ly Speaking: Debunking Ten Myths, and a Business Strategy-Informed Developmental Industrial Policy" in *New Perspectives on Industrial Policy for a Modern Britain*, Bailey, Cowling and Tomlinson. eds. Oxford: Oxford University Press.

Porter, M.E. 1990. *The Competitive Advantage of Nations*, New York: The Free Press.

Porter, M.E. and van der Linde, C. 1995. "Towards a New Conception of the Environment-Competitiveness Relationship" in *Journal of Economic Perspectives*, 9(4): 97-118.

Potter, P., and Moore, B. 2000. "UK Enterprise Zones and the Attraction of Inward Investment" in *Urban Studies*, 37(8):1279-1312.

Potter, J., Miranda, G., Cooke, P., Chapple, K., Rehfeld, D., Theyel, G., Kaufmann, D., Malul, M., and Rosenboim, M. 2012. "Clean-Tech Clustering as an Engine for Local Development: The Negev Region, Israel", in *OECD Local Economic and Employment Development (LEED) Working Papers*, 2012/11. Paris: OECD Publishing. Available at http://www.oecd.org/cfe/leed/50540391.pdf. (Accessed 26th January, 2015).

Power, J. 2012. "Local Government Reform Plan a Welcome Step' in *Irish Examiner*, 19th October, 2012.

Power, J. 2013. "Housing Strategy Essential as Market Moves", in *Daily Business Post*, 31st October, 2013.

Price Waterhouse Cooper. 2010. *Biotechnology Reinvented*. Dublin: PriceWaterhouseCooper.

Q

Quéré, M. 2004. "The Post-Genome Era: Rupture in the Organization of the Life Sciences Industry?" in *The Economic Dynamics of Modern Biotechnology*, Laage-Hellman, J., McKelvey, M., and Rickne, A., eds. Cheltenham: Edward Elgar Publishing.

Quinn, B. 2009. "Regional policy and politics" in *Europeanisation and New Patterns of Governance in Ireland*, Rees, N., Quinn, B., and Connaughton, B., eds. Manchester: Manchester University Press, 103–121.

R

Robertson, P.L., and Jacobson, D. eds. 2011. *Knowledge Transfer and Technology Diffusion*, Cheltenham: Edward Elgar Publishing.

Rose, K. 2011. "Inner City Myths: The City and its Opponents". Paper to the Humanities Institute of Ireland, UCD (unpublished).

Rosenfeld, S. 2002. "Creating Smart Systems - A Guide to Cluster Strategies in Less Favoured Regions (European Union-Regional Innovation Strategies)". Brussels: European Commission.

S

Saxenian, A. 1994. *Regional Advantage: Culture and Competition in Silicon Valley and Route 128*, Cambridge, MA: Harvard University Press.

Senker, J. 2004 "An Overview of Biotechnology Innovation in Europe: Firms, Demand, Government Policy and Research, in *The Economic Dynamics of Modern Biotechnology*, Laage-Hellman, J., McKelvey, M. and Rickne, A. eds. Cheltenham: Edward Elgar Publishing.

Sharpe, J. 1995. "Local Government: Size, Efficiency and Citizen Participation", in CDLR (Steering Committee on Local and Regional Authorities) *The Size of Municipalities, Efficiency and Citizen Participation*, Local and Regional Authorities in Europe, no. 56, Council of Europe, 63-82.

Sheridan, C. 2008. "The Elan Alumni", *The Scientist*. 7th January, 2008.

Sissons, A., and Brown, C. 2011. *Do Enterprise Zones Work: An Ideopolis policy paper*, London: The Work Foundation.

Stevenson, L., and Lundstrom, A. 2001. *Entrepreneurship Policy for the Future*, Stockholm: Swedish Foundation for Small Business Research.

Stewart, J.C. 1989. "Transfer Pricing: Some Empirical Evidence from Ireland" in *Journal of Economic Studies*, 16(3): 40-56.

Stewart, J.C. 2005. "Capital in the New Economy: A Schumpeterian Perspective" in *Entrepreneurship, the new economy and public policy: Schumpeterian perspectives*, Cantner, U., Dinopoulos, E., and Lanzillotti, R.F. eds. New York: Springer.

Stewart, J.C. 2013. "Corporation Tax: How Important is the 12.5% Corporate Tax Rate in Ireland?" in *The Nuts and Bolts of Innovation: New Perspectives on Irish Industrial Policy*, Jacobson, D. ed. Dublin: Glasnevin Publishing.

Sweeney, P. 1990. *The Politics of Public Enterprise and Privatisation*, Dublin: Tomar.

Sweeney, P. 1998. *The Celtic Tiger, Ireland's Continuing Economic Miracle*, Dublin: Oak Tree Press.

Sweeney, P. 2004. *Selling Out? Privatization in Ireland*, Dublin: Tasc at New Island.

Sweeney, P. 2008. *Ireland's Economic Success: Reasons and Prospects*, Dublin: New Island.

Sweeney, P. 2013. "State Support for the Irish Enterprise Sector" in *The Nuts and Bolts of Innovation: New Perspectives on Irish Industrial Policy*, Jacobson, D. ed. Dublin: Glasnevin Publishing.

Swianiewicz, P. 2010. "If Territorial Fragmentation is a Problem, is Amalgamation a Solution? An East European Perspective" in *Local Government Studies*, 36(2): 183-203.

T

Talbot, J. 1988 "Have Enterprise Zones Encouraged Enterprise? Some Empirical Evidence from Tyneside" in *Regional Studies*, 27:507-514.

Teece D., Pisano, G., and Shuen, A. 1997. "Dynamic Capabilities and Strategic Management" in *Strategic Management Journal*, 18, 509-533.

Temouri, Y. 2012. "The Cluster Scoreboard: Measuring the Performance of Local Business Clusters in the Knowledge Economy", OECD Local Economic and Employment Development (LEED) Working Papers, 2012/13, Paris: OECD Publishing.

Ter Wal, A., and Boschma, R. 2007. "Applying Social Network Analysis in Economic Geography: Theoretical and Methodological Issues" in *Annals of Regional Science*, 43(3): 739-756. Available at http://www.springerlink.com/content/b07154h73003756p/?p=edfd4c 687e70437b80a7e310f5bd02f1&pi=5. (Accessed 26th January, 2016).

The Green Way. 2011. *The Green Way - Dublin's Cleantech Cluster Propelling Ireland's Green Growth*. Dublin: The Green Way.

Thornhill, D. 2015. *Review of the Local Property Tax*. Available at http://www.budget.gov.ie/Budgets/2016/Documents/Review_of_Loc al_Property_Tax_pub.pdf. (Accessed 14th March, 2017).

Tideman, N. 1994. *Land and Taxation*, London: Shepheard-Walwyn.

Travers, T., Jones, G., and Burnham, J. 1993. *The Impact of Population Size on Local Authority Costs and Effectiveness*, York: Joseph Rowntree Foundation.

Trinity College Dublin. 2015. "Trinity Access Programme", Dublin: Trinity College Dublin. Available at www.tcd.ie/trinity_access/, Dublin, Trinity College Dublin. (Accessed 26th January, 2016).

Tuairim. 1960. *Papers of James Meenan – Move of UCD to Belfield*; UCD Library: University College Dublin.

Turok, B. 2008. *Wealth Doesn't Trickle Down: The Case for a Developmental State in South Africa*. New Agenda: South African Journal of Social and Economic Policy.

Tyler, P. 1993. "Enterprise Zones: the British experience" in *International Economic Insights*. May/June: 42-43.

U

UN Habitat. 2010. *State of the World's Cities Report 2010/11 Bridging the Urban Divide*, London: Earthscan.

V

Van Egeraat, C., and Curran, D. 2010. "Social Network Analysis of the Irish Biotech Industry: Implications for Digital Ecosystems", Springer Lecture Notes of the Institute for Computer Sciences, Social-Informatics and Telecommunications Engineering (LNICST) Vol. 67.

Van Egeraat, C., O'Riain, S., and Kerr, A. 2009. Social and Spatial Structures of Collaboration and Innovation in the Knowledge Economy. Deliverable 11.2 for EU FP6 OPAALS Research Project.

Vetter, A., and Kersting, N. 2003. "Democracy versus Efficiency? Comparing Local Government Reforms across Europe', in *Reforming Local Government in Europe: Closing the Gap between Democracy and Efficiency*, Kersting, N., and Vetter, A. eds. Opladen: Leske and Budrich, 11-28.

Vickers, T. 2007. *Location Matters: Recycling Britain's Wealth*, London: Shepheard-Walwyn.

W

Watts, H. 1987. *Industrial Geography*. Harlow: Longman.

Williams, B., Walsh, C., and Boyle, I. 2010. "The Development of the Functional Urban Region of Dublin: Implications for Regional Development Markets and Planning", in *Journal of Irish Urban Studies*, 7/9:5-29.

World Bank. 2011. *World Development Indicators 2011*, Washington: The World Bank Publications Office.

World Bank. 2012. *Geography of Growth – Spatial Economics and Competitiveness*, Washington: The World Bank Publications Office.

Z

Zodrow, G. R., and Mieszkowski, P. 1986. "The New View of the Property Tax: A Reformulation" in *Regional Science and Urban Economics*, 16 (3): 309–327.

Zodrow, G. R. 2006. "Who Pays the Property Tax?", *Land Lines*, 18(2).

Also Available from Glasnevin Publishing

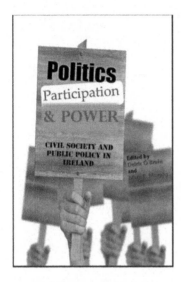

Politics, Participation & Power
Edited by Deiric O'Broin and Mary
Murphy
ISBN-13: 978-1-908689-19-1

The Nuts and Bolts of Innovation
Edited by David Jacobson
ISBN-13: 978-1908689-25-2

**Awaken the Genius Within: A Guide to
Lifelong Learning Skills**
Samuel A Malone
ISBN-13: 978-1-908689-24-5

Degrees of Nonsense
Edited by Brendan Walsh
ISBN-13: 978-1-9086891-02-3

Also Available from Glasnevin Publishing

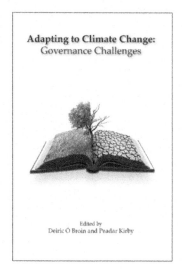

Adapting to Climate Change
Edited by Deiric O'Broin and Peadar Kirby
ISBN-13: 978-1908689-30-6

Innovation in the Social Economy
Edited by Deiric O'Broin and Mary Hyland
ISBN-13: 978-1908689-27-6

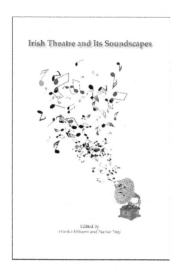

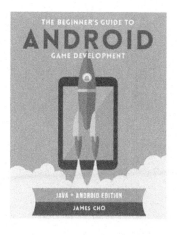

Irish Theatre and its Soundscapes
Edited by H. Mikami & N. Yagi
ISBN-13: 978-1-908689-28-3

The Beginner's Guide to Android Game Development
by James Cho
ISBN-13: 978-1-9086891-26-9

Lightning Source UK Ltd.
Milton Keynes UK
UKOW04f1007210917
309614UK00001B/30/P